Two Hours Beyond

ATLANTA

*Easy Day Trips from
the Capital of the South*

By Lincoln S. Bates

Illustrated by Bonnie Lann

Adventure Roads Travel / OCEAN TREE BOOKS

Adventure Roads Travel series:

Discovering Dixie Along the Magnolia Trail
Two Hours Beyond Atlanta
Santa Fe On Foot
Journey to O'Keeffe Country

Lincoln Bates is co-author of *Uncommon and Unheralded Museums*

Published by:
OCEAN TREE BOOKS
Post Office Box 1295
Santa Fe, New Mexico 87504
(505) 983-1412

Copyright © 1996 by Lincoln S. Bates
All rights reserved.
Printed in the United States of America.

ISBN 0-943734-27-4

Illustrations: Bonnie Lann
Cover design: Arroyo Productions
Maps: Richard Polese
Text design: John Cole GRAPHIC DESIGNER

Library of Congress Cataloging in Publication data:

Bates, Lincoln S., 1945-
    Two hours beyond Atlanta: Easy day trips from the capital of the South / By Lincoln S. Bates; illustrated by Bonnie Lann.
        p.   cm. -- (Adventure roads travel)
    Includes index.
    ISBN 0-943734-27-4
    1. Atlanta Region (Ga.)--Guidebooks. 2. Automobile travel--Georgia--Atlanta region--Guidebooks. I. Title. II. Series.
    F294.A83B38 1996
    917.58'231443--dc20   96-6892
                                  CIP

Two Hours BEYOND ATLANTA

For Brendan,

who explored many of these paths with me.

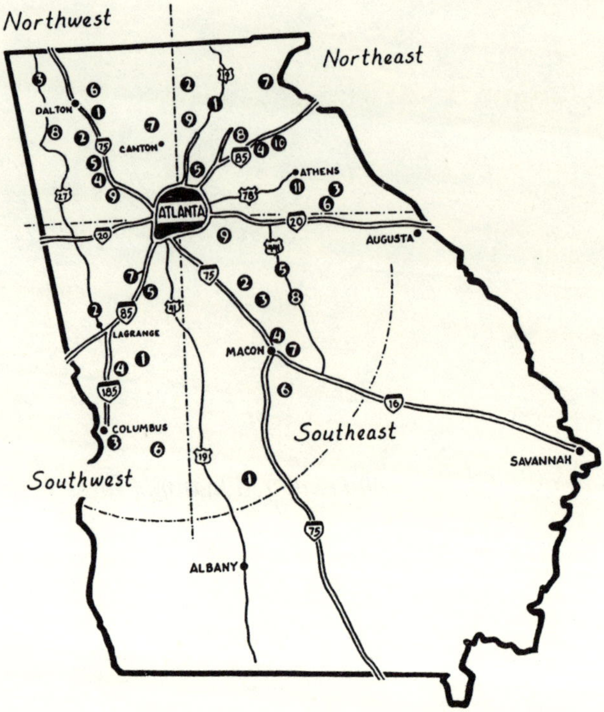
Northwest
Northeast
Southeast
Southwest
DALTON
CANTON
ATHENS
ATLANTA
AUGUSTA
LAGRANGE
MACON
COLUMBUS
SAVANNAH
ALBANY

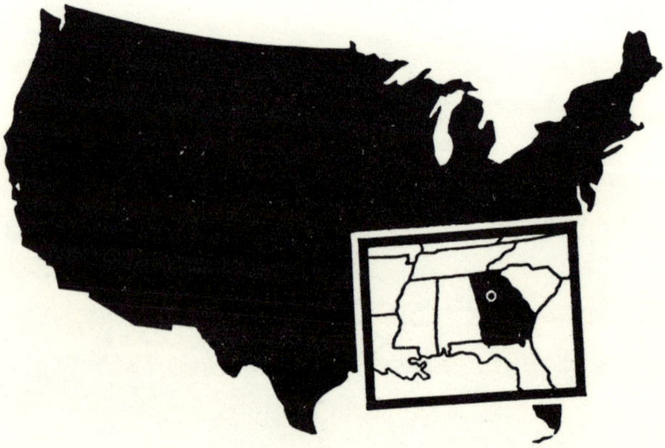

Contents

Introduction *Beyond the City* 11

Northwest of Atlanta 13
1. New Echotah *Cherokee Capital* 15
2. Barnsley Gardens *Roses, Ruins and Ghosts* 19
3. Chickamauga *Fateful Gateway* 22
4. Etowah Indian Mounds *Pieces of the Past, I* 25
5. Weinman Mineral Museum *Hard Rock Buffet* 28
6. The Chief Vann House *Showplace of the Cherokees* 31
7. The Tate House *A Winning Marble* 34
8. Paradise Garden *Vision of Another World* 36
9. Kennesaw Mountain Battlefield *The War Comes Home* 39

Here and There *Northwest* 41

Northeast of Atlanta 43
1. Dahlonega *A Glittering History* 45
2. Amicalola Falls State Park *Fair Falls and Tall Trails* 49
3. The Robert Toombs Home *Forever Dixie* 52
4. Crawford Long Museum *Medical History Made in Georgia* 55
5. Southeastern Railway Museum *All Aboard!* 58
6. Alexander Stephens Home *On the Path of Duty* 60
7. Tallulah Falls *Taking the Plunge* 63
8. Georgia's Wine Country *Fruit of the Vine* 66
9. The Bill Elliott Racing Museum *Life in the Fast Lane* 69
10. The Commerce Connection *Shop Till You Drop* 72
11. Butts-Mehre Heritage Hall *How 'Bout Them Dawgs!* 75

Here and There *Northeast* 77

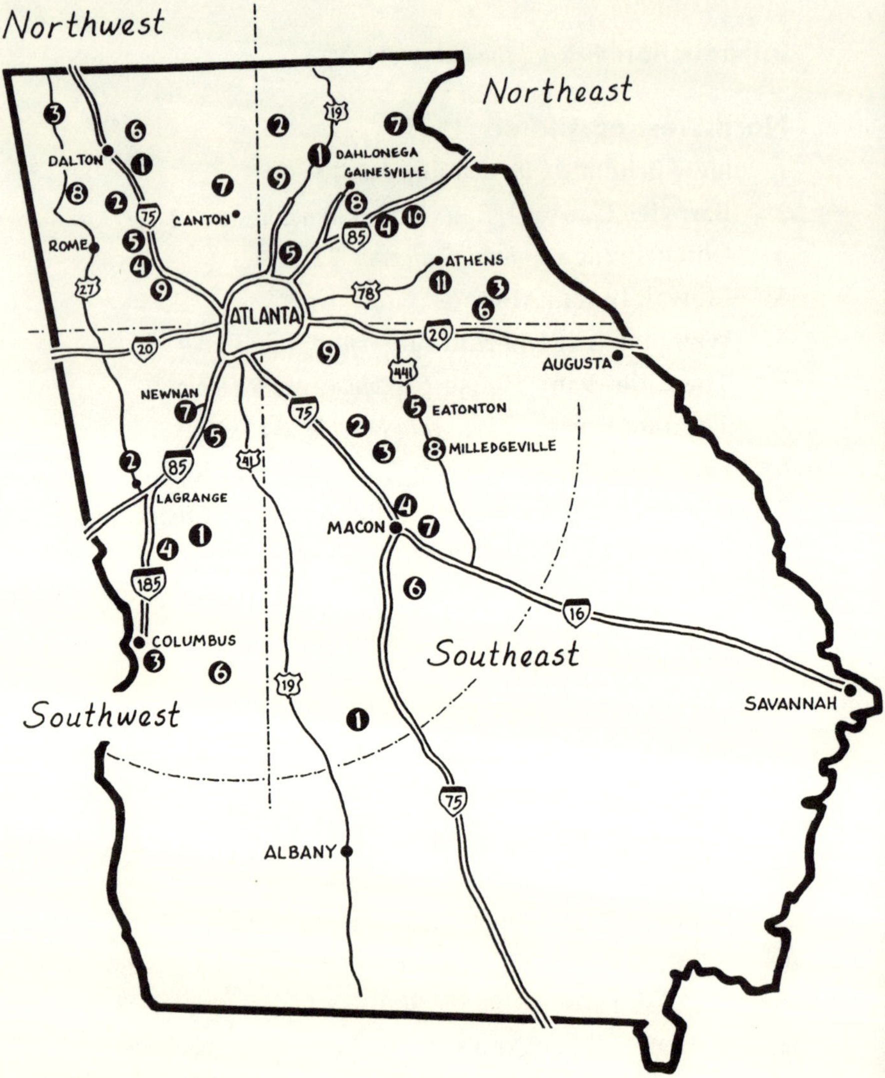

Northwest
Northeast
Southeast
Southwest
DALTON
ROME
CANTON
DAHLONEGA
GAINESVILLE
ATHENS
ATLANTA
AUGUSTA
NEWNAN
EATONTON
MILLEDGEVILLE
LAGRANGE
MACON
COLUMBUS
SAVANNAH
ALBANY

Southeast of Atlanta 79
1   Andersonville *Portrait of POWs* 81
2   Piedmont National Wildlife Refuge
     More than an Animal Shelter 85
3   Jarrell Plantation *Down to Earth* 88
4   The Hay House *History in the Makin'* 91
5   Eatonton *A Rabbit Runs Through It* 94
6   The Museum of Aviation *Flying High* 97
7   Ocmulgee National Monument *Pieces of the Past, II* 100
8   Milledgeville *A Capital Idea* 102
9   Panola Mountain *Back to Nature Nearby* 105
    Here and There *Southeast* 108

Southwest of Atlanta 111
1   The Little White House *FDR's Georgia Retreat* 113
2   Bellevue *A Manor to Which You're Accustomed* 117
3   The Confederate Naval Museum
     Ironclads and Iron Will 120
4   Callaway Gardens *Butterflies Flutter By* 123
5   Erskine Caldwell Birthplace *Author's Little Acre* 127
6   Buena Vista *State of the Arts & Music* 130
7   Newnan *An Education in Architecture* 134
    Here and There *Southwest* 136

Back in the City *A Few Suggestions* 137

Index *Attractions and Events* 141

Introduction

Beyond the City

FROM blues bars and upscale eateries to science museums and professional sports, Atlanta has much to offer visitors whether they're in the city for a few hours or a few days, for the Olympic Games or a weekend getaway.

But for those with a little time to spend and a desire to journey beyond the urban confines and perhaps go deeper South, there are diverse doings and surprising sights at all points of the compass and within two hours of town.

The Civil War, its echoes ever reverberating in the region's consciousness, is never far away. Spots such as Kennesaw Mountain, Pickett's Mill and Chickamauga enable you to revisit the carnage and courage of that epic struggle. Georgia's early days are elegantly reflected not by some fictional *Tara* but in the truly historic homes of Macon, Madison, Newnan, Washington and LaGrange. Native American heritage beats strongly at New Echotah and other sites a short distance from Atlanta.

For more contemporary tastes, visit Georgia's growing wine country northeast of the city, savor peach products throughout the southern marches, and sample apples and cider along the sides of northern county roads. Paradise Garden and Pasaquan are among offbeat regional curiosities. Botanical beauty beckons in places such as Callaway Gardens and Barnsley Gardens. Cool, green nature paths are as close as Sweetwater Creek and Panola Mountain or as far as Amicalola Falls near the southern terminus of the famed Appalachian Trail. Seasonal festivals and fairs abound here, calling up a rich heritage of music, crafts and cuisine.

From Franklin D. Roosevelt's retreat southwest of the city to gold mining north of Atlanta, from medical pioneering to folklore and storytelling, from a myriad bargains to minor league baseball and serene woodland walks—it's all but a short day trip away.

INTRODUCTION

Each of the four quadrants in this guidebook contains several principal destinations, complete with information on travel time, hours open, fee (if any) and phone number. And each major section concludes with a roundup of miscellaneous sights, sounds and flavors of the region. Four maps facilitate location and identification of the main entries. A fifth section offers some personal favorites in Atlanta itself.

Selecting which quadrant to explore first, or choosing spots within a sector, may depend on the weather, available time, and your personal inclinations. In north Georgia, especially in the mountains, the air runs a bit cooler. The landscape there is more vertical, the scenery more varied, the pathways and byways a little more demanding. You typically travel farther to reach points in the southeast and southwest quadrants, so allow more road time for treks in those directions. No quadrant really has a monopoly on subject matter, but Civil War and Native American sites most likely take a northwest tangent. If you're after architecture, Madison and Washington lie to the east of Atlanta, Newnan and LaGrange to the southwest, Milledgeville and Macon to the southeast. But whichever way you go, you can't go wrong.

These trips focus on a place rather than a trek, but in some cases getting there is part of the fun. In other cases, it's possible to visit more than one place in a single outing. And if you've the time and inclination to dally, off the interstates are flea markets as abundant as fleas, oddball roadside attractions, scenic views, and regional delicacies such as Southern barbecue and boiled peanuts. Just reading communities' names on the road map—Zebulon, Flowery Branch, Kansas, Bogart, Madras, Sonoraville, Panthersville, Stevens Pottery, The Rock, Pobiddy Crossroad—is a trip.

In short, this book gives you a wealth of destination options—but the journey is up to you. Get yourself a road map of Georgia (the AAA map and the official one from the Department of Industry, Trade and Tourism, 404/656-3590, are excellent.) One caveat: although this information is as up-to-date as possible, schedules and admission fees are subject to change. Calling ahead first is advised.

That said, welcome to the world surrounding metro Atlanta. Happy travels!

Lincoln S. Bates

Northwest of Atlanta

NORTHWEST QUADRANT

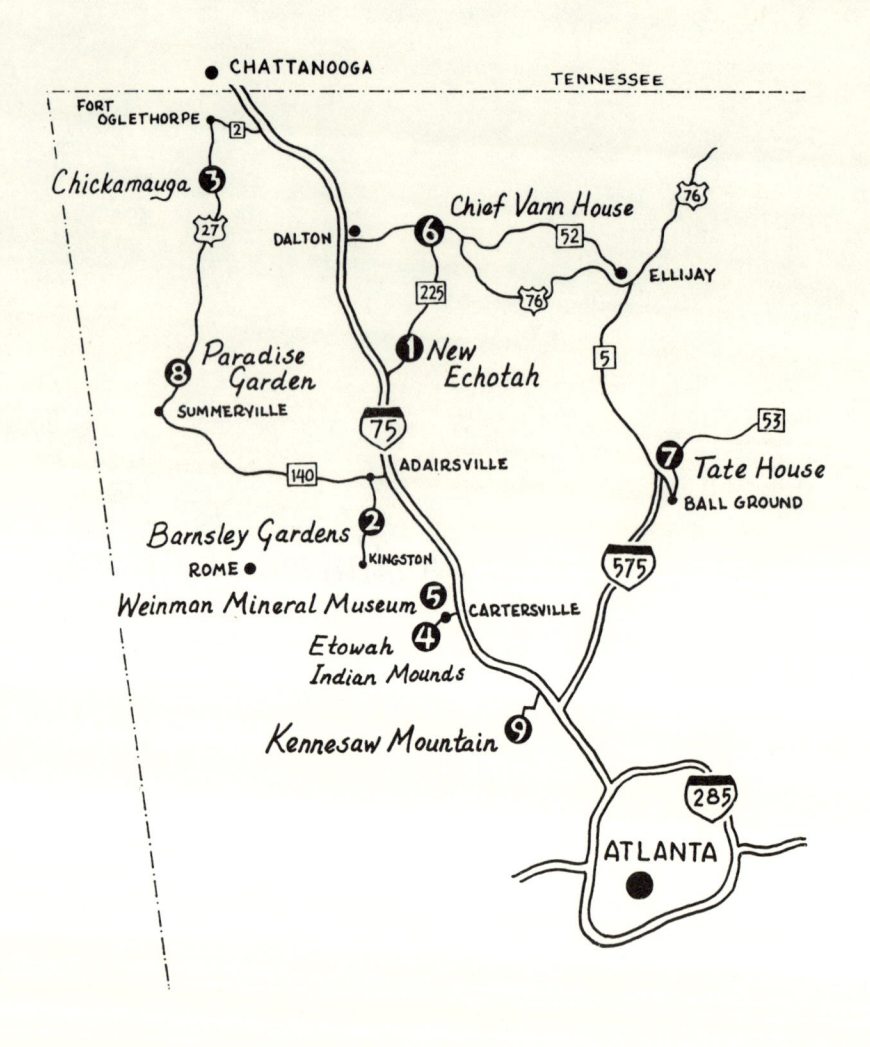

(1) New Echotah
(2) Barnsley Gardens
(3) Chickamauga
(4) Etowah Indian Mounds
(5) Weinman Mineral Museum
(6) The Chief Vann House
(7) The Tate House
(8) Paradise Garden
(9) Kennesaw Mountain Battlefield

1. New Echotah

Cherokee Capital

THE meadow simmers in a warm Southern sun, its resident buildings starkly etched against the grassland. Scores of Cherokee voices once rippled across this fruitful ground, talking of crops, commerce, laws and living, and of pressure from encroaching whites. The place stands quiet now, but nonetheless tells a sobering story.

In the early 1820s, the Cherokee Indians—seeking acceptance from and equality with an expanding Anglo culture—adopted a republican form of government and passed laws for support of schools, repair of roads and regulation of liquor. They established a capital in north Georgia that, among other things, housed their supreme court and a print shop which published a weekly newspaper.

New Echotah was short-lived. In the mid-1830s, President Andrew Jackson's administration and the Georgia state government drove the Cherokees from their ancestral lands in the Southeast, banishing them to Oklahoma along the infamous Trail of Tears.

But today you can visit this former capital and get a glimpse of the town as it stood 160 years ago, with several structures restored or replaced and others in the planning. An adjacent highway and a neighboring golf course offset any sense of time travel, but strolling about the 200-acre site reveals how closely, and futilely, the Cherokees emulated whites. It reflects a peaceful, prosperous, adaptable people seeking coexistence in a rapidly changing land.

A visitors center and small museum introduce you to the site with a short video presentation, dioramas and displays of artifacts. Self-guided walkabouts are encouraged; guided tours take a bit more time and offer more information.

Supreme Court Building

A freeze-frame quality characterizes New Echotah now, but what the town represents looms larger than the community itself. Even in its day, the town was small, numbering perhaps 75 to 100 perrmanent residents, typically families raising vegetables, cotton and tobacco. But legislative sessions, which occurred several times throughout the year, could swell the population to a couple of thousand.

No council house now occupies the spot where the legislature once convened, but nearby stands the reconstructed **supreme court building**, a two-story, white-clapboard edifice where cases from circuit and district courts across the Cherokee nation were heard. Inside, you find an elevated bench for three judges and another six benches for those involved in the proceedings.

The **Vann Tavern**, an early 1800s Cherokee structure, moved to the site from Gainesville, Georgia in 1955, authentically represents the type of inn that offered food, drink and lodging in New Echotah. The pine timbers are weathered yet solid. A huge stone fireplace dominates the kitchen and adjoining first-floor room. Whiskey, beef, cornmeal and beans were served at a long pine table. One sign reads: *"Room & board 25c. Clean sheets 10c."* A prototypical take-out window at the rear handled drive-through trade. "It was for slaves, troublemakers and drunks," notes a site attendant. "They wanted their money but not their presence."

In a wooded glade 100 yards or so from the town square stands the **Worcester House**, two-story residence of the Reverend Samuel Worcester and the original community's only surviving structure. The clapboard house, with its double-decker veranda, served as church, school and post office. Wonderfully restored, it contains period implements and furnishings such as a loom, spinning wheel, laundry and cooking gear, writing desk and rope bed. One unusual feature is closets, rare for that time and place.

The middle of New Echotah's spacious meadow holds the site's central attraction, a replica of the **print shop** where between 1828 and 1834 Elias Boudinot edited and produced *The Phoenix*, a four-page newspaper printed in English and Cherokee. Boudinot printed 200 to 300 copies weekly. The paper ciruclated not only to Cherokee villages in the Southeast but to U.S. and European cities as well. Guides run off sample pages for visitors, one benefit of the escorted tours. The actual press is period equipment, but the original was seized by state militia in the 1830s.

Contemporary Cherokees reportedly had no input in reconstructing New Echotah— retrieved from corn and cotton fields in the 1950s—although tribal documents indicated layout and pro-

Print Shop

vided data on specific structures. But Cherokees do revive New Echotah each fall when tribal members from North Carolina convene at the old capital and recreate a bit of life as it was in their forefathers' day. The annual **Cherokee Festival**, which began over a decade ago, involves traditional dances and songs, pottery, basket weaving, weapons demonstrations, storytelling, and games. Cherokees wear full ceremonial dress for the dances. The event also presents a ball game and a blowgun competition.

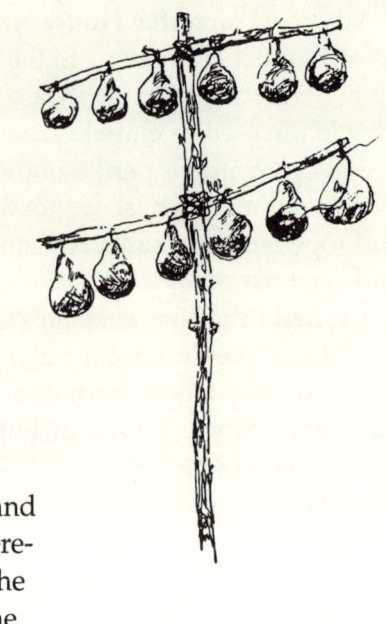

The festival is not so much for Cherokees as it is for the general public, to observe and learn, says one Cherokee who has helped stage the event. "We try to keep it as historic and authentic as we can through games, crafts and language."

The federal government plans a national historic trail to mark the Trail of Tears through nine states. New Echotah does not lie on the trail itself; however, the establishment of that route may raise the profile of this once-thriving government and communications center. But it won't change New Echotah's value as a history lesson for us all.

New Echotah lies about one hour northwest of Atlanta on I-75. Take exit 131 and go right on Route 225. The site is open year round Tuesday through Saturday 9 a.m. to 5 p.m., Sundays 2 p.m. to 5:30 p.m. Admission is $1.50 for adults, 75 cents for children. Telephone: 706/629-8151.

2. Barnsley Gardens

Roses, Ruins and Ghosts

IN the 1820s, a handsome young Englishman married a lovely Savannah lass, and he built for her a garden estate amid the wild, forested hills of northwest Georgia. Alas, she died before the manor was finished, but her spirit returned and advised him on construction and decor. Later, war came and wiped away the family's wealth. Eventually, the mansion fell into disrepair, and still later internecine murder stained the manorhouse.

Backdrop to a romance novel or plot for a made-for-TV movie? Possibly, but here it's the stuff of history, too. And you can revisit the events by visiting the ruins, now called Barnsley Gardens, not far from Atlanta. Botanical beauty, a trove of family treasures and various special events make it more than a love story among the ruins.

Godfrey Barnsley made his fortune in shipping and the cotton trade in Savannah, Mobile and New Orleans. When his wife, Julia, contracted tuberculosis, he felt an uplands climate might benefit her, so he purchased thousands of acres of vacated Cherokee land in Bartow County. He began construction in 1841, only to see Julia die four years later. But, with the help and inspiration of her ghost, so the story goes, he pushed on and completed the family manor, called *Woodlands*, in 1856. It boasted marble window facings, hand-sculpted mantels, elegant wall paneling, even running water with flushing commodes. His ships brought back furnishings and plants from around the world.

The main building today is a brick shell fronted by towering trees and a boxwood *parterre* in the center of which stands a 12-foot-tall fountain. Rose bushes, butterfly bushes and other plants ornament the garden. Within the walls, you can still see door frames, ceiling beams, fireplaces and a brick vault where Godfrey kept his documents and gold. In what had been the drawing room a five-arch window overlooks a side garden.

A wing that once served as kitchen, servants quarters and billiards room now houses a small museum which details the family history and lifestyle. There are numerous photos of the manor dating from the last quarter of the 19th century and of relatives and descendants representing branches of the family tree. Display cases contain goblets, books, a writer's pouch, fans, land deeds and Godfrey's personal shaving gear. One room exhibits clothing, quilts, a marriage license, baby book and more old photos. The kitchen holds a unique built-in rotisserie stove designed by Godfrey and manufactured in England.

The basement of this wing once stored bottles of brandy and wine. Now, one room shows a short video on the history and restoration of the estate. A neighboring room displays Civil War uniforms, weapons and gear, plus paintings of battles in the area. Over the past 60 years, cartridge boxes, powder pouches, canteens and firearms have been found in the surrounding acreage.

As delightful as savoring the Barnsley story may be, you'll find equal enjoyment strolling the pathways that wind through 30 acres of grounds. A bog garden and fernery beckon from the bottom of the south-sloping hill. Farther afield, you find an Oriental garden, a wildflower meadow and a copse of rhododendron. In spring, azaleas and thousands of daffodils brighten the landscape. Roses, hundreds of them, grace arbors and fences; indeed, the family motto is "Life is like the rose." Numerous benches encourage rest and contemplation.

Hubertus Fugger-Babbenhausen, a German prince, purchased the property in 1988 and launched an extensive restoration of the gardens and grounds, devised the museum, added a nursery and gift shop and opened the place to visitors in 1991. Special events include a daffodil fest in spring, gardening workshops, a Civil War encampment, and a cotton jamboree in early fall. In mid-October, there's a day focusing on "the spirits of Barnsley."

Barnsley Gardens lies about an hour northwest of Atlanta between Kingston and Adairsville. Take I-75 north and get off at exit 128. Go west on Route 140, then south on Hall Station Road. Go west again on Barnsely Gardens Road and follow it about two miles; the site is on the left. It's open March 1 through November 1, Tuesday through Saturday 10 a.m. to 6 p.m. and Sunday noon to 6 p.m., and November 2 through February 28, Tuesday through Saturday 10 a.m. to 4:30 p.m. and Sunday noon to 4:30 p.m.; closed Mondays and the month of January. Admission is $6.50, seniors $5.50, under 11 free. Guided tours are available for groups of 10 or more. Telephone: 770/773-7480.

3. Chickamauga

Fateful Gateway

As the third year of the Civil War staggered to a close, Confederate forces grudgingly lost ground. It seemed difficult, if not impossible, to turn tactical triumph into real advantage.

At Chickamauga, just below the Tennessee rail hub of Chattanooga, Confederate troops under General Braxton Bragg battled Union forces at close quarters for two bloody days in September 1863. They hurled the Federals back but failed to retake the city, earning a hollow victory. Two months later the resupplied Union army again advanced, knocking the rebels off Lookout Mountain and Missionary Ridge. The next spring, Sherman began his fateful drive on Atlanta.

In 1890, at the urging of veterans from both sides, Congress established the Chickamauga Battlefield Park to commemorate their courage and honor the dead. This, the first and largest military park, above all symbolized the beginnings of reconciliation.

Today the place is a peaceful spot, and at first glance would seem simply that—a park—but for the cannons and markers starkly punctuating meadows and woods. Deer graze in some of the fields. Horseback riders appear through the trees. Bicyclists flash along narrow roads. It's an excellent place for a picnic lunch, but also for sobering reflection.

The approach to the park is a commercialized contrast, a lengthy and bustling strip mall. But you know you're getting close when you pass Battlefield Centre and Battlefield Elementary School and see signs for "Battlerama."

At the visitors center you're greeted by bellicose batteries of period cannon, grim iron barrels mounted on wooden wheels giving the impression they're still looking for a fight. Inside, wall panels sketch the start and course of this internecine war that, for better or for worse, shaped the nation. There are dioramas, maps

CHICKAMAUGA

and artifacts—some you might expect, such as a mobile forge that helped keep a pre-mechanized army moving; and some you might not, for instance a tree trunk from the battleground still embedded with 12-pound cannonballs.

Adding a martial layer is the **Fuller Gun Collection**, exhibiting three centuries of firearms in America—from Spencer repeaters to Hill breech-loaders, from Springfields to Kentucky long rifles—more than 350 weapons in all. In a way, it aptly reflects the land of the free and the home of the well-armed.

A must at the center is the compelling 24-minute multimedia presentation, *The Battle of Chickamauga*. Shown in a partial wraparound theater, it weaves veterans' reminiscences and dialogue with the story of the battle, replete with scenes from diaries, paintings and re-enactments. Shifting, startling, engulfing, a bit confusing (not unlike the battle), it recounts the struggle in an informal, conversational way, and it dutifully offers perspectives of both sides.

The two-day struggle produced 34,000 casualties, and a seven-mile drive through the park (with or without audio cassette rental) conveys the quieting/disquieting feeling of visiting a cemetery. More than 600 stone and bronze monuments were erected between 1890 and 1930. The Union regimental markers identify places where units from Michigan, Ohio, Illinois, Indiana and Wisconsin saw their heaviest fighting; Confederate markers, representing Georgia, South Carolina, Florida and Alabama brigades, note farthest points of advance. Some markers are tightly clustered, resembling graveyard headstones, while others stand apart like lonely sentries. One of the most striking is an 85-foot-tall limestone tower with crenellated battlement built in 1903. At Snodgrass Hill stands another company of markers, these signaling the spot where General George Thomas blunted the Confederate breakthrough, saving the Federals from a shattering defeat and earning him the sobriquet, "The Rock of Chickamauga."

The fighting surged back and forth through dense woods, tangled vines and thick underbrush. Some units lost half their men in a single day of combat. One Confederate commander report-

NORTHWEST OF ATLANTA

edly called Chickamauga Creek "a sluggish river of death." In the end, the Southern forces slammed the gate but couldn't lock it. Sherman's army soon forced its way through and headed for Atlanta, then Savannah and the sea.

To reach Chickamauga National Military Park, take exit 141 off I-75 north, go west on Route 2, then south on U.S. 27. Driving time from Atlanta is one hour and 45 minutes. Admission is free, but the multimedia show costs $2.25 for adults and $1 for children and seniors. The park is open daily 8 a.m. to 5:45 p.m. in summer months and till 4:45 p.m. after Labor Day; closed Christmas. In late spring and during the summer the park hosts encampments and demonstrations; call for a schedule of events. Telephone: 706/866-9241.

4. Etowah Indian Mounds

Pieces of the Past, I

THE southside of Cartersville, Georgia seems an unlikely archeological zone. You drive through a leafy residential neighborhood, past a public school, along a road flanked by upscale subdivisions. Then, as the road drops down toward the graceful Etowah River, in an idyllic meadow you arrive at the remains of a Native American culture that, like many others, gives the lie to celluloid stereotypes.

Beyond the small museum and a broad ditch loom three huge, grass-covered mounds, casting historic shadows over the fringes of exurbia. There's not a little irony at this state-managed site. Across the road rests a cemetery called Sunset Gardens Memorial Park, and abutting the acreage is the Bow & Arrow Mobile Home Park. Cows graze in a pasture to the east. To the northwest, you can spot three chimney stacks of a power plant belching smoke.

But here the entire setting is placid and park-like. Quite likely, it was a rather peaceful place 500 to 1,000 years ago when people of the widespread Mississippean culture dwelt here— farming, hunting and trading. The 50-acre town, which may have numbered 2,000 residents at its peak, was laid out around a plaza. The large mounds served as platforms for homes of chieftan-priests, as temples and as mortuary houses. Upper-class types and selected belongings were buried in the mounds. Material for these flat-topped, four-sided knolls came from pits and ditches around the site. The ditches, connected to the river, also served as a defensive moat inside which once stood a palisade of logs.

Staple crops for these people, possibly related to later Creeks or Cherokees, consisted of sunflower, pumpkins, corn and beans grown in the fertile soil along the river. They also dined on persimmon, walnuts, hickory nuts and meal made from acorns.

Catfish, gar and mussels came from the river, and ample game was available in the nearby forests. The bottomland provided cane for thatch, baskets and mats.

A pathway directs visitors to the three mounds. Another path follows the river. Several smaller mounds dot the edge of the former *plaza* or town square. Wooden stairways permit ascent to the tops of the trio of prominent knolls, the tallest of which is Mound A at 63 feet. This vantage point gives a proper perspective of the site.

Principal excavations by the Georgia Historical Commission and the University of Georgia occurred in the mid-1950s. Partial work on Mound B turned up the secular and routine—bone tools, pottery shards, animal remains. But Mound C produced scores of burials, revealing information on diet, dress, disease and customs. The mound was built up in layers, with changes in temple structures and burial practices dating from earliest at the bottom. Mound A remains intact.

The museum, housing more than 500 artifacts, exhibits the site in microcosm. There's a diorama of house construction. Arrow points and traps indicate the type of hunting employed. Other items from the digs reveal a wonderful richness. For example, you see stone ceremonial bowls and ritual pipes, as well as stone and copper axes. Forelock beads, ear discs and copper insignia reflect the ornamental side of this society. Excavation also has produced conch shell *gorgets* and bowls, pearl and wood beads, effigy jars and a copper-covered wooden rattle. A separate display shows how goods such as salt, shells and obsidian were traded among various North American Indian peoples.

Among the most striking artifacts displayed are two 125-pound human figures discovered at the edge of Mound C. The pair were finely fashioned from marble without the use of iron tools and painted red, black, green and white. The haunting figures—a seated male and kneeling female—may represent memorial statues or mortuary images of village VIPs.

A centerpiece of the museum is a reproduction burial pit containing the remains of a 16th-century chieftan-priest, realistically reflecting a find in Mound C. Of more modern vintage is a slide show illustrating the importance of conserving archeological sites.

Etowah Indian Mounds is reached via I-75 north, taking exit 124 onto Main Street heading west to Cartersville. Follow the signs about five miles. The site is approximately 40 minutes from Atlanta. It's open Tuesday through Saturday 9 a.m. to 5 p.m., Sunday 2 p.m. to 5:30 p.m. Admission is $2 ages 19 and over, $1 ages 6 to 19. Telephone: 770/387-3747.

5. Weinman Mineral Museum

Hard Rock Buffet

ROCKS may be silent, but they speak with great beauty—at least when polished and presented as they are at this mineral museum northwest of Atlanta.

Named for William Weinman, an early barite miner in the region, the museum shows several facets of Georgia's minerals, and in particular the mining of them. The low-slung, single-story building is bounded on one side by large chunks of rock and some earth-moving equipment. Near the entrance stands a Hardinge conical mill used by Weinman to water-grind the first calcium carbonate in the United States. Inside, there are black-and-white photos of local barite and manganese mining operations and a life-size diorama of a grizzled miner sitting outside his cabin surrounded by hammer, pick and other tools of his trade.

The museum also counts exhibits on granite and kaolin, two of the state's important commercial minerals. The former, of course, plays a big role in construction. The latter, a fine clay, goes into paints, porcelain and paper. Georgia claims some of the world's richest kaolin deposits.

One exhibit room not only displays dazzling gemstones such as garnet, topaz, olivine, spodumene and jadeite, but also has an ersatz limestone cavern which illustrates how such cavities are formed by leaching water, eroding rock and deposition. You'll also see Pleistocene fossils of a ground sloth and an extinct peccary, as well as petrified wood and a 375-million-year-old shark's tooth.

You view various forms of barite and there are amythest crystals the size of your fist, accompanied by a recounting of the 1930s Charlie's Creek amythest strike up in Towns County.

Quartz takes many forms. In addition to the usual pink and white varieties, there are amythest, bloodstone and jasper, among others.

You'll also see samples of the state's official mineral—*staurolite*, often called fairy crosses or fairy stones due to the dark twinned crystals that form crosses or partial crosses. Believed by some to be good-luck charms, they reportedly can often be found at Hackney Farm in Fannin County near where Georgia, North Carolina and Tennessee meet. (Gemstone prospecting is something of a cottage industry in parts of north Georgia.)

Much of the material resides in cases, but large chunks of calcite are eminently touchable, and there's a certain sensuality in caressing a geode.

In the Mayo Wing stand cabinets and cases of gloriously colored and polished minerals; indeed, the room is nothing short of an art gallery. You see stunning rhodochrosite in pink, coral and red. One case is devoted to galena or lead ore, some pieces in gray cubes, others rubbed and rounded and looking like silver beads. Another case offers beautiful green jade in the form of fruit, flowers and knife handles. Elsewhere in the wing you find a piece of amythest as big as a nightstand and a Southwestern sunset on the surface of a polished piece of petrified wood.

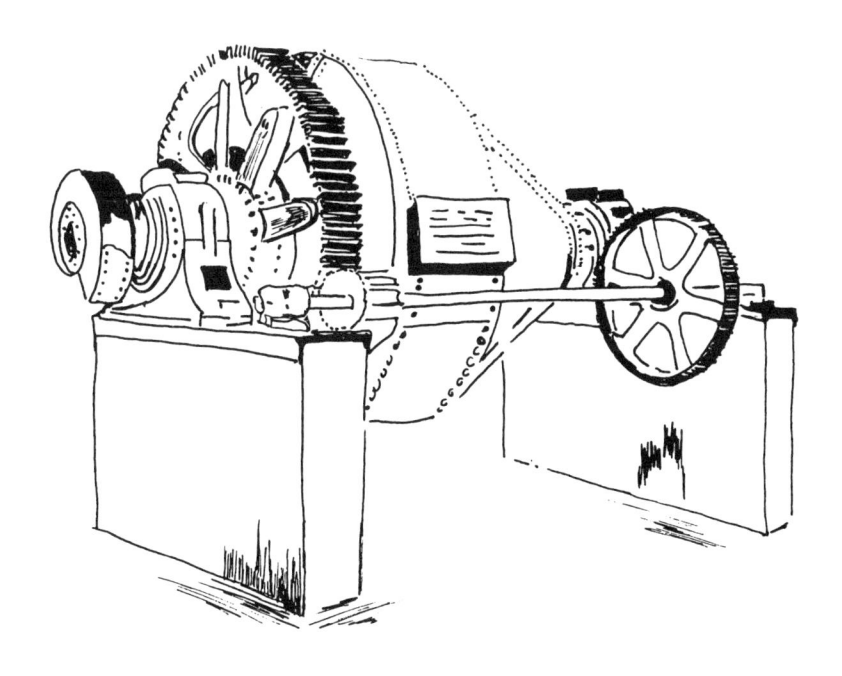

NORTHWEST OF ATLANTA

The museum shows videos on mining in Georgia, on rocks and minerals, and on volcanoes, and it sells various rock-related items. Annually on the second weeknd in June, it hosts a "rock swap" where dealers buy and sell and rockhounds attend in droves. Among other special events are lapidary exhibits and a fancy-gemstone competition.

The Weinman Mineral Museum in Cartersville is off exit 126 of I-75 north. Go left at the bottom of the ramp; the museum is on the west side of the interstate. Driving time from Atlanta is about 45 minutes. It's open Tuesday through Saturday 10 a.m. to 4:30 p.m., Sunday 2 p.m. to 4:30 p.m.; closed Monday. Admission is $3 for adults, $2.50 for seniors, $2 ages 6 to 11. Telephone: 770/386-0576.

6. The Chief Vann House

Showplace of the Cherokees

A FEW miles east of Chatsworth, Georgia and not far from the apple capital of Ellijay, on a grassy knoll overlooking forests and fields, stands the Chief Vann House, a two-story, red-brick manor built in 1804. Its Federalist lines, columned porticos, classic cornices, tall windows, and rich interior give an unaccustomed view of American Indian life—even more dramatically than the Cherokee hub of New Echotah.

Erected by James Vann, a wealthy half-Cherokee, half-Scot who sponsored a Moravian mission school to educate Cherokee children, the house was the showplace of the Cherokee nation. It originally commanded some 800 cultivated acres (4,000 total), a sawmill, foundry, smokehouses, barns, cabins and orchards, plus scores of slaves. Time and events have whittled the once-proud plantation down to the house and a couple of dozen acres of grounds.

It's not evident now, but a history of violence attends the place. Vann was fatally shot in a Cumming, Georgia tavern in 1809. His son Joseph inherited it but was forced out in the mid-1830s when whites began to appropriate Indian land. The immediate pretense for eviction was that Vann had hired a white man to work for him, which was against the law. Reportedly, two whites, arguing over claim to the property, subsequently had a shootout in the central hallway.

Between then and 1947 the house had some 15 owners, and perhaps more than 100 people lived there over the years as the grand manor deteriorated. In 1952 the county historical society bought the place from Dr. J.E. Bradford and deeded it to the state, and the historical commission restored the structure inside and out. Today, the house is as imposing as ever, although one attendant wonders how long it can withstand heavy visitation.

The Moravians helped build the house and a German architect named Vogt was brought in to design it. The missionaries' diaries yield considerable information about construction of the place. It's now furnished with period (1780-1840) antiques and reproductions.

The first and second floors each contain two rooms of about 600 square feet apiece and separated by a central hallway. The third floor holds two children's rooms—with six-foot-high ceilings, a couple of bureaus, small tables and beds—on the east and west sides of the house.

On the second floor you find the adults' bedrooms, both equipped with fireplaces and four-poster beds. The guest bedroom, on the west side, contains settees while the other has a small table on which rest a wine decanter and playing cards. A wooden holder with a clay pipe in it hangs by the fireplace. A cantilevered stairway with hand-carved trim connects the first two stories, and a spinning wheel and loom occupy the the second-floor landing. The stairs reportedly represent the oldest cantilever construction in Georgia.

The ground-floor rooms consist of the dining area on the east side (food was brought in from an external kitchen) and across the hall the drawing room, complete with an 1825 piano and 1790 grandfather clock, across the hall. Here you see "Christian doors," the panels supposedly representing open pages of the Bible and their centerpieces a cross. The hinges were made in the Vann blacksmith shop. One of the more striking features of the drawing room is the five-foot-wide parlor fireplace with mantelpiece that reaches the ceiling. Panels and moldings in the room bear original hues—blue for the sky, red for the Georgia clay, green for the grass and trees, and yellow for the ripened grain.

Exhibit cases in the first-floor hallway display artifacts found at the site—horseshoes, coins, arrowheads, a hatchet head, pottery shards, a file, utensils, nails, an original lock, Joseph Vann's gold-seal ring, land titles, and other items.

The Chief Vann House is located at the intersection of Route 52 (U.S. 76) and Route 225, best reached via I-75 north (using exit 136), about an hour and a half from Atlanta. It's open year-round (except Christmas and Thanksgiving) Tuesday through Saturday 9 a.m. to 5 p.m., Sunday 2 p.m. to 5:30 p.m.; closed Monday. Admission is $2 for adults, $1 for kids. Telephone: 706/866-9241.

7. The Tate House

A Winning Marble

IT'S not what you might expect to see in the rolling, rural hills of north Georgia: a polished stone of a home amid the kudzu patches, auto graveyards, faded dwellings, and metal-roofed barns. It could almost be a mirage.

But the Tate House, built in 1923-1926 by the man who consolidated several small firms into the Georgia Marble Co., is as real and solid as the rare pink marble from which it was made. Once the family manor, it has since become a mini-resort. The main house is a bed and breakfast, and posh-looking log-style cabins (equipped with fireplaces and hot tubs) some yards away near the tennis courts provide additional rooms. A small, kidney-shaped pool and attractive terrace and formal garden flank the east side; on the other are a greenhouse and antique shop. You can go horseback riding across the road, and canoeing on the Etowah River is only 12 miles away. But you don't have to stay the night or even lunch here to walk through it and appreciate how the upper crust once lived in north Georgia.

Stephen Tate began mining marble in the region in the late 1800s and his son Sam solidified and expanded the industry in 1917. He built the pink marble mansion as a family home and a showcase for his product. However, the Depression rocked the company. Neither Sam nor his brother Luke, nor sister Flora, married, so there were no direct heirs. The house eventually fell vacant and remained so for a quarter century. Vandals stole the furniture and moonshiners erected a still in the upstairs. Ann Laird discovered the place in 1974, and restored the mansion to its former grandeur. It was opened to the public in 1985.

The massive three-story, colonnaded edifice, with its lustrous marble exterior, has something of the cast of a bank, memorial or government building. You enter at the west portal. On the left is

THE TATE HOUSE

a sitting room blending the past and present—a large-screen TV and Indian blankets, dolls and decorative arts. Dark wood molding plays off the smooth marble floor, marble-bordered fireplace, and expansive octagonal table topped with tiles.

Across the hall is a bedroom with crystal chandelier, four-poster bed and ornate cabinets studded with cameos. The lower half of the entire bathroom is marble as well.

The wood-paneled ballroom seems suitable for dancing or lounging, and weddings do a big business here. An interesting arrangement on one wall comprises mounted china casserole tops on the left panel and a built-in cabinet on the right. This room sweeps into the spacious dining area where a small alcove overlooks garden and terrace. Nearby is the winter kitchen.

Back in the center of the house, you ascend a graceful curving staircase to the second floor. Wallpaper throughout the hallway/staircase depicts idyllic, Mediterranean-like scenes.

Four bedrooms occupy the upper floor—Luke's, Colonel Sam's, Miss Flora's, and the Jewel Room—each distinctively and differently done and each with its own marble-lined bath.

On the lower level, you find the summer kitchen, and through it you come to a cozy den on the walls of which hang numerous photos showing what the place looked like before, during and after renovation (one shot calls to mind a Mayan ruin in Yucatan).

Further along is the former garage, now a pub with masculine wood and brass bar and an enclosed addition for extra tables. This area is topped by the terrace which promises to be most romantic in moonlight.

The Tate House lies about an hour's drive north of Atlanta via I-75 and I-575. Beyond Ball Ground, turn right onto Route 108 which becomes Route 53 at an intersection. Follow Route 53 east past an old railroad depot. The house is on the right just before you reach the marble plant. You can usually tour the house Monday through Friday 9 a.m. to 8 p.m.; on Saturday and Sunday it depends on how busy the place is. Fee for tours is $2. Call for information about rooms and restaurant or on the place in general. Telephone: 770/735-3122.

8. Paradise Garden

Vision of Another World

AFTER U.S. 27 winds out of Rome, Georgia it courses through Summerville en route to Chattanooga, Tennessee, where the spectacular new aquarium now eclipses traditional tourist stops such as Rock City and Ruby Falls. But a few hundred yards off old 27 just north of Summerville, in a place called Pennville, sits one of the most amazing roadside attractions in north Georgia or southeastern Tennessee—Howard Finster's Paradise Garden.

It's not a garden in the English or Japanese sense (nor in the Callaway or Barnsley style). Indeed, some might view it as a flea market gone berserk, a scrap heap of civilization or a singular commentary on the relationship of God, man and machine. Finster, a preacher, self-taught artist and self-described "stranger from another world," inscriptionally says of it: "I built this park of broken pieces to try to mend a broken world of people who are traveling their last road."

Why stop? One, this four-acre plot in the midst of a neighborhood of mobile homes, matchbox houses and aging American-made cars is like nothing else in these parts. Two, every step is a discovery. Three, it's free. And four, Finster is not your average artisan.

In 1976, so the oft-repeated story goes, a face appeared in a smudge of paint and directed him to "paint sacred art." This preacher/repairman with a sixth-grade education obeyed, and soon his drawings, paintings, cutouts, and sculptures propelled him into the big time and big bucks—some pieces running into five figures. His work has appeared in galleries and museums from London to L.A. and has illustrated ads, magazines and rock albums. He believes his inspiration comes from God and that art is a vehicle for preaching.

PARADISE GARDEN

Finster began the garden in 1961 at age 46 when he moved here from nearby Trion where he'd built a prototype he called a roadside park museum. Today, this bizarre melange of discards, makeshift monuments, structures, signs, cutouts and assemblages seems nothing less than a visual stream-of-consciousness evangelical sermon with strokes of humor, love and redemption.

A sidewalk embedded with shards of glass and ceramic leads visitors past the studio and into the garden. Along the wall you see portraits on fabric of Jesus, Elvis and others, plus a bit of folksy Finster biography. And don't be surprised at numerous self-portraits on the way. He invites photography: "You can carry my work out to many people by your own camery [sic] pictures and copies on cards or poster," one sign declares.

Ahead is a three-story, several-sided, steeple-topped edifice bedecked with metallic spangles and scriptural passages. Nearby is a wire-mesh locomotive threaded with beads, vines and coiled wire. The path heads left where you see a white Cadillac partially covered with the faces of Jesus, JFK, Abraham Lincoln, the Mona Lisa and a host of lesser luminaries, and the notation, "The Dead and Living Come Together."

Plants flower in old-fashioned tub washers. A huge pile of coils, bars, bicycle parts and twisted tubing is held together and embraced by living vines. Near a five-foot-long high-top shoe sculpted of white-painted concrete stands a decrepit shed with faded "Love It or Leave It" posters and a "God Is My Co-Pilot" sign. Over a row of rusted cash registers hangs a bomb inscribed, "Their Shall Be Wars in Last Days."

There are enough old, broken appliances to energize the Maytag man. Wasted refrigerators hold no sustenance, containing instead worn shoes, a cracked ceramic cat skull, a metal cannister, chunks of rock, an explosion of vines.

The deco sidewalk continues, studded with marbles, bullet shells, locks, keys, razors, horseshoes and more. Stubby towers glisten with inlaid shards and bulge with figures of birds, snakes, rabbits and human faces both horrific and holy.

Structures become sculptures in this fantastical realm. For example, a shed on stilts has exterior walls made of mirrors instead of standard shingles. With trees in the background and mirrors reflecting foliage, it creates the vaguely unsettling effect of making you think you're looking through the building. An elevated corridor holds posters, thank-yous, photos, exhibition announcements, writeups, and artwork.

Whether Finster is wacky or wise, supernatural or very natural, is perhaps in the eye of the beholder. But his son and grandson are following his artistic path, and he has made his colorful mark here in Pennville, in Atlanta and beyond—possibly farther than we (but not he) dare imagine.

Pennville is just above Summerville, about one hour and 50 minutes from Atlanta. Take I-75 north to Adairsville and proceed west on Route 140 until it joins U.S. 27. Take that route north through Summerville and about two-and-a-half miles out of town, just after the Pennville Church of Christ, go right on Rena Street between two auto supply stores and follow it back a couple of blocks—you can't miss Finster's place. There's no charge to stroll through Paradise Garden. It's open Monday through Friday 10 a.m. to 5:30 p.m., noon to 6 p.m. on weekends.

9. Kennesaw Mountain Battlefield

The War Comes Home

WITH the passage of years, an uncommon calm settles over battlefields, a peace surpassing that of other landscapes. Perhaps it is the span of time, perhaps the contrast between then and now, perhaps the healing and the restoration, but it's a fitting quietude.

Kennesaw National Battlefield Park, just northwest of Atlanta, reflects that sort of peace. The air is lighter, clearer; the wildflowers appear brighter; the shade cooler. The very earth seems softer, more forgiving. Here you can picnic without hassle, read or reminisce, toss a football or a Frisbee, fly a kite, work a tan, and exercise your legs and imagination.

It wasn't always so serene. In June 1864, Kennesaw Mountain howled with the agony of war as Union and Confederate forces struggled yet again in a long and bloody conflict that would redefine the nation.

The Union campaign to take Atlanta—a foundry and transportation hub—began at Chattanooga, Tennessee in early May. General William T. Sherman marched his 100,000-man army southeast, opposed by General Joseph E. Johnston and 65,000 Confederate troops. Tough, veteran soldiers filled the ranks of both sides.

Rocky Face Ridge. Resaca. New Hope Church and Pickett's Mill. Sherman forced Confederate retreats with a series of flanking maneuvers. In mid-June he confronted the rebels at heavily fortified Kennesaw Mountain, two dozen miles from Atlanta and three miles north of Marietta.

Between June 19 and July 2 the hills and fields shuddered with artillery barrages and several brief but savage skirmishes. Some of the fighting was hand-to-hand. The North lost 3,000 men and the South 800. Sherman flanked yet again, and Johnston's troops withdrew to protect the railroad and their supply lines. The Union grip reached for Atlanta's throat.

Not a major battle like Gettysburg or Shiloh, Kennesaw nonetheless exemplifies the Union drive for Atlanta. According to one park attendant, for the federal government it is *the* representative site of the Atlanta campaign. The park was established in the late 1930s and dedicated to both the battle and the entire campaign. Today, the site combines history with outdoor recreation and welcomes people from east and west as well as North and South.

Period cannon stand sentry in a field at the foot of the 1,800-foot-high ridge. A split-rail fence surrounds the vast meadow that hosts numerous demonstrations and events, including infantry maneuvers, cavalry charges and artillery firings. Also on the interpretive schedule, which runs April through October, are topics such as Sherman's March and women and blacks in the War Between the States. There's also an evening program highlighting facets of the conflict.

Inside the compact visitors center you'll find books, maps and an auditorium which provides a brief orientation to the battle and the park. A small exhibit room displays banners, uniforms, weapons and gear typical of the Atlanta campaign.

The site, however, offers more than a history chapter. A chief attraction of **Kennesaw Mountain** is the many miles of hiking trails that wind through the forest. The most popular trace takes a one-mile, 40-minute switchback route to the top of the ridge where in a northerly direction you can see rolling fields and distant hills and almost spy Sherman's advance. To the south, on a clear day, you can view downtown Atlanta, its glass-and-steel spires representing a far different city from the one Sherman assaulted more than 125 years ago. Along the trail, you notice an old rifle pit and now-silent cannon still wheeled into position. (A vehicle road also takes visitors to a small parking lot below the summit.)

Other trails lead from the top of the ridge down toward **Little Kennesaw** and **Pigeon Hill**, about five-and-one-half miles round trip from the visitors center. It's also possible to hike all the way to **Cheatham Hill** and **Kolb's Farm**. The former was the site of fierce fighting during the battle—soldiers fell quickly at the spot they nicknamed the "Dead Angle." Kolb's Farm is a restored 1836 farmhouse that became the headquarters for Union General Joseph Hooker. These latter trails are 10 and 16 miles round-trip, respectively.

Wildflowers and birds punctuate the woodsy setting, as do monuments to the fallen. The hiking is easy to moderate—some steep hills—and the weather in summer is invariably hot and humid. It's a good idea to take along water for the longer trails.

Kennesaw Mountain Battlefield Park is open daily year round except Christmas. Hours are 8:30 a.m. to 5:30 p.m., and admission is free. About a 30-minute drive from Atlanta, the park is easily reached off I-75 at exit 116. Go left and travel about six miles, then turn right on Cobb Parkway and left at the first traffic light. Telephone: 706/427-4686.

Northwest Quadrant

Here and There

EN route through northwest Georgia, where the clouds hang low on the humpbacked hills, consider other Civil War-related locales. One is **Pickett's Mill**, not far from Kennesaw Mountain, a state-run site recounting a prelude struggle to Kennesaw itself. Also near Kennesaw is **Big Shanty Museum** which features *"The General,"* a railroad engine used in the Andrews Raid, a bit of derring-do made into a movie called *The Great Locomotive Chase*. Farther north, off I-75 near Dalton, is the town of **Tunnel Hill**, so named because of a 1,400-foot-long railroad tunnel Union forces captured in its drive on Atlanta; remains of the tunnel are still there even if Yankee soldiers are not.

Just outside Chatsworth stands 2,800-foot-high **Fort Mountain**, named for a large stone-wall formation dating back at least a millenium. Some think it's the work of wandering Welsh mariners, but most authorities credit Native Americans.

In Rome, visit the **Martha Berry Museum** on the lovely campus of Berry College which contains an art collection and memorabilia associated with Miss Berry and the school. Also in Rome is the **Chieftains Museum**, former home of Cherokee leader Major Ridge.

In Cartersville just off I-75 is a **Budweiser brewery**, built in 1993, which welcomes visitors who wish to learn how one of the leading beers in the United States is made. If you prefer non-alcoholic, you can explore a small limestone cavern in Cave Springs south of Rome and drink cool, clear water right from the spring.

At **Reinhardt College** between Canton and Tate, the entire main campus is an arboretum containing many rare species of trees and shrubs, plus a nature trail.

In season, sample the **Prater's Mill Country Fair** in Dalton (May), the **Georgia Marble Festival** in Jasper (early October), and the **Georgia Apple Festival** in Ellijay (October).

Northeast of Atlanta

NORTHEAST OF ATLANTA

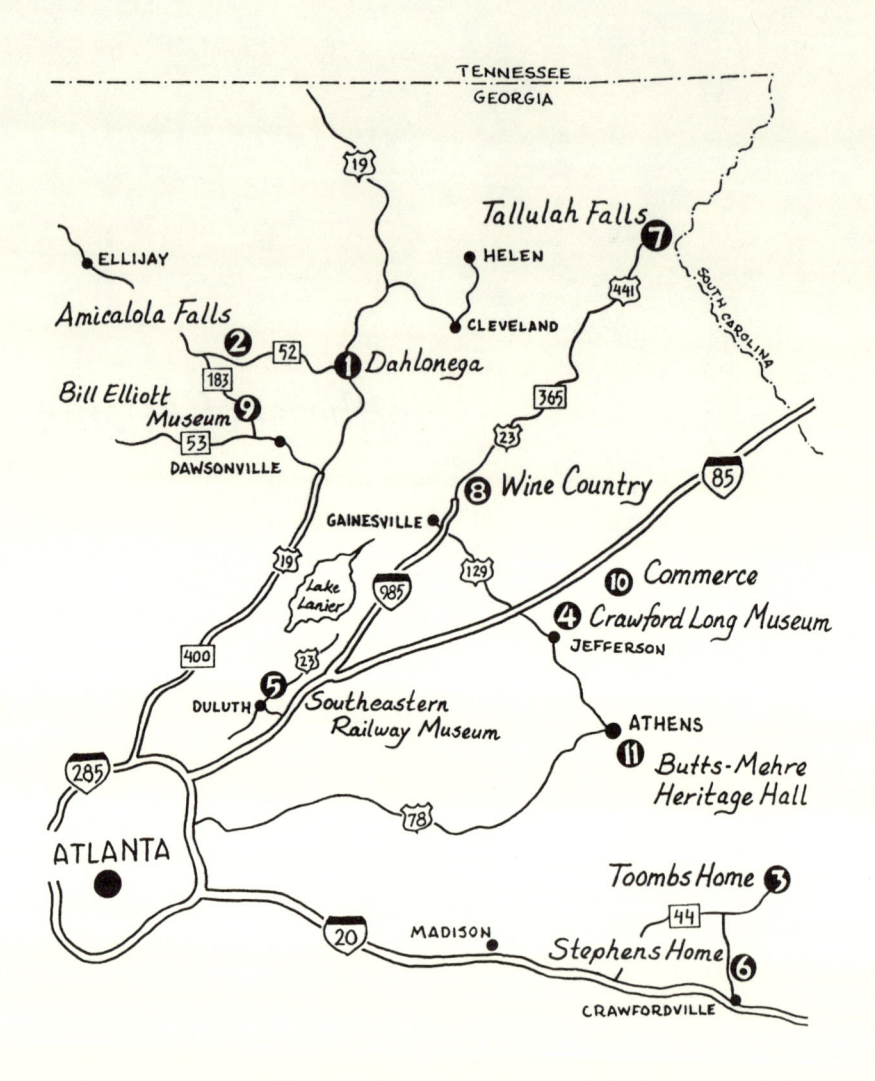

(1) Dahlonega
(2) Amicalola Falls State Park
(3) The Robert Toombs Home
(4) Crawford Long Museum
(5) Southeastern Railway Museum
(6) Alexander Stephens Home
(7) Tallulah Falls
(8) Georgia's Wine Country
(9) The Bill Elliott Racing Museum
(10) The Commerce Connection
(11) Butts-Mehre Heritage Hall

1. Dahlonega

A Glittering History

IN 1828, so the story goes, Benjamin Parks found gold in the north Georgia hills, an event that triggered the nation's first gold rush. The discovery of gold on what was then Cherokee land lured thousands of fortune hunters to the verdant mountains.

Dahlonega, the Lumpkin County seat, occupies the heart of Georgia's gold country and the old county courthouse today is a museum that recounts the history of gold mining in the region. This two-story red-brick structure stands in the middle of the town square, partly surrounded by balconied 19th-century buildings. The original bricks, made from local materials, reportedly contain tiny grains of gold. Erected in 1836, it's Georgia's oldest public building north of Atlanta.

The second floor offers an excellent introduction to gold hunting in north Georgia and to the building itself. An exhibit case displays artifacts and mementos—a fiddle, pistol, mining company records, newspaper clippings, photos, even a 1942 issue of *Life* magazine that featured the courthouse. The jury room, judge's chambers and a clerk's rolltop desk claim part of the space. There's also an old water cannon from the hydraulic-mining era.

Behind a large curtain you'll find seating for a 25-minute video that carries viewers through more than century of gold prospecting here and brings the lure of gold to life via commentary from fourth-generation miners and family members. There was a lot of hardship involved and most folks never struck it rich, but there's no cure for gold fever, one elderly woman observes.

You learn that the federal government established a branch mint at Dahlonega in 1838 which produced more than $6 million in gold coins, a fraction of the gold mined in north Georgia.

In the early days gold filled the stream beds, but miners turned to digging veins in the 1840s. Some 30 years later, hydraulic mining—high-pressure water blasts—ripped apart the hillsides. Later came deep-shaft mining. Thundering stamp mills crushed the ore and chemicals extracted the gold. The names of the mines clink like nuggets in a tin cup—Cane Creek, Calhoun, Barlow, Whim Hill, Jumbo and Keystone—and the waterways ripple in the sun: Etowah, Yahoola, Chestatee. It's said that Georgia gold is among the purest in the United States.

The museum's first floor, which some decades back housed doctor' and lawyer' offices and a restaurant, is divided into three rooms displaying dioramas, mining gear and some of the precious metal itself. A massive safe, weights and measures, a crucible, a turn-of-the-century stamp mill, and panning tools give the story a three-dimensional cast.

Dahlonega doesn't give up on gold. For modest fees ($2 to $3), you can pan for gold at **Crisson Mine**, **Consolidated Mine** and the **Smith House**, among other local spots—and for free in streams flowing through public lands such as the nearby **Chattahoochee National Forest**.

An interesting spin on the story of north Gerogia's gold is the **Consolidated Mine** not far from the Gold Museum. Once the site of the biggest gold mining operation east of the Mississippi River, the place now mines visitors' curiosity. They have reopened a tunnel some 185 feet below ground, one of perhaps 200 tunnels that burrow through the bedrock. A 45- minute tour provides an uncommon glimpse of a most hazardous job. Knowledgeable guides point out gold-bearing quartz veins and old mining tools unearthed in the shaft. You learn about drilling techniques and "dynamite headaches." And you may see a bat or two clinging to the overhead rock.

Held in April at Consolidated is the annual World Championship Gold-Panning Competition which in 1988 moved to Dahlonega from California.

Speaking of the Golden State, there's another story from Dahlonega that illustrates east is east and west is west and...well, in 1849 Matthew F. Stephenson, assayer at the mint, tried to dissuade miners from heading to California. Orating from the courthouse steps, he gestured to the surrounding lofty landscape and cried, "There's millions in it!"—a phrase later transformed by author Mark Twain into "There's gold in them thar hills!"

Dahlonega and its 24-carat sites are easily reached via Georgia 400 (a toll road) and U.S. 19, about an hour north of Atlanta. The Gold Museum is open all year (except major holidays) Monday through Saturday 9 a.m. to 5 p.m., Sundays 10 a.m. to 5 p.m. Admission is $1.75 for adults and 75 cents for kids. Telephone: 706/864-2257. Consolidated

Mine is open seven days a week, 10 a.m. to 4 p.m. Admission is $7 for adults, $4 for kids (price covers a pan of gravel to prospect). Telephone: 706/864-8473.

2. Amicalola Falls State Park

Fair Falls and Tall Trails

THE verdant north Georgia hills are laced with sparkling creeks and waterfalls, many of them easily accessible to the weekend tourist and casual hiker. DeSoto, Duke's Creek, Anna Ruby, Panther Creek and others delight the eye and ear and somehow soothe the soul.

Among the most lovely of the region's cascades is Amicalola (Cherokee for "tumbling waters") Falls, almost due north of Atlanta and just west of the former gold capital of Dahlonega. Part of Georgia's extensive state park system, Amicalola is clean, green and inviting.

A multifaceted park, Amicalola offers guest cottages, campsites, restaurant/lodge, picnic and playground area, trout fishing and trails through trees. You can drive or hike to the top of the falls, the latter a one-and-a-half mile uphill trek that takes 45 minutes to an hour. The shorter **West Ridge Trail** meanders through dogwood, rhododendron and mountain laurel on the other flank of the falls and ends up at the walkway to an observation platform near the waterfall's base. Here you gaze up through the foliage and watch the pearly stream tumble down the 729-foot-high cliff.

The hiking is moderate, but it's wise not to push yourself too hard in the humidity of summer. Even the climb to the observation deck is a bit steep. Along this path you'll find informational plaques about indigenous plants and animals. One of these is titled, "Who Cooks for You?" a phrase resembling the call of the great horned owl. The barred owl, explains the marker, makes a similar call but with a Southern accent—"Who Cooks for Y'all?"

The park offers special seasonal events such as a spring flower hike and an October foliage display, backpacking clinics and trips, and a summer presentation on mountain lore and legend.

An added feature of Amicalola Falls is its proximity to **Springer Mountain**, the southern terminus of the **Appalachian Trail**. This famed wilderness pathway, proposed by Benton McKaye in 1921 and opened in 1952, winds some 2,000 miles from north Georgia to Mount Katahdin in Maine, passing through 14 different states. It's maintained by 32 local outdoors clubs and carries up to four million backpackers and hikers on some portion of it each year. Approximately 175 hardy souls hike the entire length annually.

Myron H. Avery, instrumental in developing the trail, wrote of this longest marked footpath in the world, "Remote for detachment, narrow for chosen company, winding for leisure, lonely for contemplation, it beckons not merely north and south, but upward to the body, mind and soul of man."

An approach trail of eight-and-a-half miles climbs up to 3,782-foot-high Springer Mountain from Amicalola Falls State Park, a hike of about eight hours round trip for the experienced and fit. An alternative route for those wishing to leave a transitory footprint on this great trail is to drive 45 to 50 minutes from the park to a small parking lot nearly a mile from the summit. It's a well-kept trail from there to the top; still, insect repellent and appropriate shoes are advised. Along this stretch, you see ferns, wildflowers, moss- and lichen- covered boulders, gnarled trees, an occasional salamander and, on a clear day, some marvelous vistas.

At the summit, you find a plaque reading, "A Footpath for Those Who Seek Fellowship with the Wilderness." A metal drawer in a rock holds a log book and pen.

This option adds about three hours to your day, but the drive (map and directions are available at the Amicalola visitors center) takes you through north Georgia apple country and past poultry farms, Baptist churches and vendors of boiled peanuts, cider and quilts—all part of the region's tapestry. The last seven miles of this route consist of a dirt-and-gravel road that snakes through the forest, but a four-wheel-drive vehicle is not necessary.

AMICALOLA FALLS STATE PARK

Appalachian Trail hikers should register at the Amicalola visitors center; indeed, they must register if leaving or parking a car there. Information about and reservations for campsites and cottages at Amicalola Falls State Park can be obtained by phone.

Amicalola Falls State Park is open daily 7 a.m. to 10 p.m. A $2 per-vehicle fee is charged (camping and cottages are additional). From Atlanta take Route 400 (a toll road) to U.S. 19 and that to Dahlonega. Turn onto Route 52 west and follow it to the park. Travel time is about an hour and a half. Telephone: 706/265-8888.

3. The Robert Toombs Home

Forever Dixie

BUMPER-STICKER communication is as common in the South as anywhere else (with the possible exception of California), but you'll find certain expressions unique to the region. A prime example is a stars-and-bars backdrop with the defiant words, "Forget? Hell, No!" If Robert Toombs were alive today, he might well sport one of these on his buggy.

A moderate and a Unionist turned ardent secessionist, Toombs represented Georgia in the House and Senate, resigning from the latter in January 1861 as the North and South split asunder. His restored home in Washington, Georgia tells much about the man and his times.

Born in 1810 near Washington, Toombs attended the University of Georgia (then Franklin College) from which he was expelled in 1827 for drinking and fighting. He eventually graduated from Union College in New York and began practicing law back home in 1830. He was a passionate, sometimes profane fellow—a lawyer, planter, orator and poet— and he naturally gravitated to politics.

Toombs opposed the Mexican War and he labored hard to keep Georgia from seceding in 1850. But he joined the Southern radicals a decade later, and he coveted the presidency of the Confederacy. He served briefly in the Jefferson Davis cabinet, in the Confederate Congress, and in the army as a brigadier general. He subsequently attacked the Davis administration for its prosecution of the war. On May 11, 1865, Union cavalry approached his home to arrest him. He slipped out the back while his wife delayed the troops and he hid amidst the north Georgia hills. Toombs then went into exile in Cuba and France.

He returned in 1867, but refused to apply for a pardon, and he came to symbolize an unrepentant South. Reportedly, he once left his calling card at the White House on a visit to President Andrew Johnson. Johnson, seeing him quickly depart, sent someone after him. He then asked Toombs why he came to visit and only left his card. Toombs replied, "I always leave my card when I visit a foreign country." He cursed compromise and carpetbaggers, and boasted of his disloyalty to the *other* Washington until his death. He also opposed railroad barons and industrial monopolies. His final years left him blind, broke and alone.

The state purchased the house in 1973, intending to restore and interpret the site. In a nice bit of irony, a 1976 federal grant of $80,000 enabled archeological work and restoration to begin. The effort continues today, but much has already been accomplished.

Four Doric columns line a narrow portico in front. Above it is a small balcony from which Toombs addressed the townsfolk. The colonnaded portion is a facade added by Toombs. The clapboard structure dates back to 1797, a two-story Federalist home built by Dr. Joel Abbot from Connecticut. The original walkway, with a stone grist wheel set in it, extends from a streetside oak tree to broad front steps.

The ground floor houses a small interpretive museum on Toombs, exhibiting family photos, canes, newspaper clips and political cartoons, a copy of the Georgia ordinance of secession, and other items. Also here is the original kitchen which Toombs converted to a law office. Nearby, a 17-foot-deep dry well stored food at a constant 52 degrees Fahrenheit. This level also offers space for viewing a 25-minute video, a dramatized period interview of Toombs by a young journalist.

The furnishings plan on the first and second floors was based mainly on an inventory taken at Toombs' death in December 1885. The living room contains Toombs family furniture, and a portrait of one daughter hangs over the mantel. Sliding doors open onto the entranceway. Opposite is Toombs' library, replete with his books and sword. Of note here as well are gas lamps imported from France, a fine secretary and two large ship's lanterns.

The dining room has sky-blue walls (the original color) as well as the Toombs' dining table. Lace curtains are puddled at the bottom, a sign of wealth. A dumb waiter in the abutting pantry brought food up from the warming kitchen; actual cooking took place in a separate building in back.

Family bedrooms hold interesting features, such as silver toiletry items in Mrs. Toombs' room and in her husband's room a small pine desk that comes apart for traveling. An armoire in the upper hallway emits a faint whiff of tobacco, for the plant was used to ward off moths.

On this floor, too, Toombs kept a room ready for his friend and colleague Alexander Stephens from nearby Crawfordville, just as Stephens maintained a room for Toombs. The original bed and other furnishings seem to stand ready for Stephens' arrival. And doubtless he made good use of the lazy-lawyer bookcase, a freestanding, four-sided shelf that rotates on a pedestal. It was a gift to him from Toombs.

Stephens reportedly once said of his friend that Toombs could rule the continent if he had more self-control and self-discipline. Reinforcing that point is a statement attributed to Toombs: "A man moderate in life is a jackass."

To reach the Robert Toombs Home, take I-20 east to exit 53 and follow Route 44 north through Greensboro to Washington. Go past the Route 44 spur, and in town at the stop sign turn right on Robert Toombs Avenue. Follow it through the business district; the house is on the right next to the Episcopal Church. Travel time from Atlanta is about one hour and 45 minutes. The site is open Tuesday through Saturday 9 a.m. to 5 p.m., Sundays 2 p.m. to 5:30 p.m.; closed Monday, Thanksgiving and Christmas. Admission is $1.50 for adults, 75 cents for kids under 18, under 5 free. Telephone: 706/678-2226. (NOTE: the **Alexander Stephens Home,** *also open to visitors, is about 21 miles south via Routes 44 and 22.)*

4. The Crawford Long Museum

Medical History Made in Georgia

PAINLESS surgery is a relatively new procedure. For centuries people suffering from wounds, disease or injuries endured still more pain during what passed for medical treatment. An arrow or musketball might be extracted on the spot. Alcohol and other potions may have helped block the pain in some situations, but their administration was hardly the stuff of science.

On March 30, 1842, Georgia physician Crawford W. Long performed the first operation using ether as anesthesia to remove a cyst from the neck of a patient. He subsequently amputated fingers and toes using the same procedure. Anesthesia, and medicine in general, has advanced considerably in 150 years, but that intial step and the man who took it are wonderfully recaptured in Jefferson, Georgia, about an hour northeast of Atlanta.

A two-story red-brick edifice, built by Dr. J.B. Pendergrass circa 1879, houses the Crawford Long Museum, one of four anesthesia-related museums in the United States. Two adjoining structures help place it in context. Entering through the smaller building, you see exhibits of Jackson County—a cotton gin, old photos—and temporary displays. The latter may entail patent medicines popular a century ago and touted for everything from diabetes to constipation to "female ailments," or some of Dr. Long's medical gear, such as his mortar and pestle.

The main exhibit room, open, airy and well-lit, contains numerous family items—a table, a cradle, children's chairs, and Long's rocker; indeed, one entire case is devoted to his family and his youth. Among the interesting artifacts are courtship letters written between Long and his wife-to-be, Mary Caroline Swain.

Here, too, reside scales, pharmaceutical jars, medical kits and instruments. Dividing the room into thematic halves is a detailed diorama of the operation that eventually made Long famous.

You learn as well that a clue to the discovery involved the practice of University of Pennsylvania medical students taking social snorts of laughing gas. Long, an alumnus, substituted ether back home in Georgia and noticed that those who fell or otherwise suffered bumps and bruises felt no pain.

On the other side of the diorama is an exhibit relating the history of anesthesia from ancient times through more modern developments such as inhalers, syringes and intravenous lines, as well as presenting cultural alternatives such as acupuncture needles. There's a 1920s anesthesia machine with imprecise gauges, a 1930s Connell apparatus, and a 1980 model. Manufacturers and hospitals donated the devices.

The upper floor houses a dozen anesthesia machines of various vintages as well as diverse masks and inhalers plus medical texts from a century ago. Up here too you can view a 1953 *Fireside Theater* presentation of Dr. Long's use of ether, a documentary film and a video of a play called *Spit of the Devil*.

The first floor offers a bit of time travel in the form of a replica of an 1840s doctor's office and pharmacy. An evolving exhibit, it has shelves of jars and canisters, drawers for raw herbs, a pill-silver to coat pills, a pill-rounder to shape them, a pocket case of small lancets, a tooth key, mortar and pestle, and a small table once owned by Long. One of the most intersting and informative items is an 1837 fee schedule of the Georgia Medical Board. No postal billing, no insurance. Removing tumors cost $10 to $60. "Extirpating hemerhoids" $5 to $25. Vaccinations for whites cost $6, for slaves $3 (or $24 per dozen). And a house call in the country after dusk had a $2 tab. Listed also were fees for visits to ships, for midwifery and for surgery.

In a nearby display case, you find Long's saddlebags containing wooden boxes filled with bottled medicinals and a Civil War-era amputation kit complete with saw, scalpels and tourniquet.

The connected white clapboard building is largely a reconstructed 19th century general store with diverse items reflecting local history, and it helps illustrate what the town was like when Long practiced here. Articles range from plows, kettles and tobacco twists to a corn sheller, coffee mill and old mail buggy.

THE CRAWFORD LONG MUSEUM

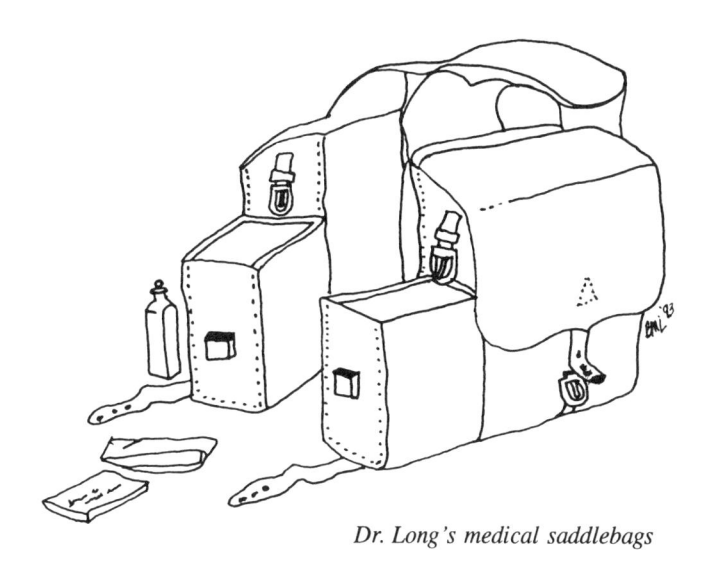

Dr. Long's medical saddlebags

Located about 60 miles from Atlanta, the Crawford Long Museum is best reached via I-85 north. Take exit 50 onto U.S. 129. Go right and travel about five miles, turning left at the middle of town where you'll find it situated on the left. The museum is open year round Tuesday through Saturday from 10 a.m. to 1 p.m. and 2 p.m. to 5 p.m., Sundays 2 p.m. to 5 p.m. Admission is free but donations are welcome. Telephone: 706/367-5307.

5. Southeastern Railway Museum

All Aboard!

RAILROADS run powerful tracks through our national memory, and this 15-acre, hands-on, outdoor museum stokes up nostalgia in fine style. The place is more impressive by its 75 units of rolling stock—the real steel thing—than by any slick layout or gadgetry. Many of the rail cars seem rusty shadows of their former selves, but others are well-preserved and some welcome you to climb aboard.

There are three Pullman cars on display, including the 1911 *Superb*, one of the earliest steel cars made. It had five bedrooms, a kitchen, a parlor and servants' quarters. The car served as the mobile home of President Warren G. Harding on a whistle-stop tour from Washington, D.C., to Tacoma, Washington, and it later became his funeral train. A walk-through of the Atlantic Coast Line's *Washington Club* reveals the faded elegance of a bygone era.

Hop aboard a bright red Southern Railroad caboose and inspect the utilitarian living quarters/office with its Union stove, toilet, closet, sink, bench compartments and elevated seats for viewing the track and train outside.

You also see industrial rail cars, such as a crane and a pile driver. One intriguing engine is a stubby, muscular locomotive bearing the name Campbell Limestone Co. which once labored for a South Carolina quarrying firm.

There are no guides, not a lot of direction nor much in the way of informational signs, but photo ops and the smell of creosote abound, and you can hear the shriek of whistles, feel the rumble of wheels, hear the clang of metal couplings and see billows of smoke when some these iron horses get into gear.

The **Comer Shop** is a working repair and maintenance barn redolent with the smell of paint and grease where you might see some actual restoration on a car or locomotive in progress. And nearby sits the depot for a 7-1/2-inch gauge mini train that transports visitors around a mile of track, giving them a different perspective of the railway museum. It's run by a local hobbyist club called the North Georgia Live Steamers.

Among other well-preserved pieces on the museum's grounds are locomotive No. 21 from the Chattahoochee Valley Railroad Co., a silvery Buddliner, a red-wheeled steam tractor, and a U.S. Mail Railway Post Office car. The latter holds the museum's collection of hundreds of books, publications and railroad memorabilia such as posters, timetables, lanterns, signal gear, rail spikes and more. Eventually the museum plans to move these materials to a climate-controlled 1,200-square-foot depot for better storage and display.

Between April and October on the third weekend of each month, the Southeastern Railway Museum holds its "steam up" days, offering short rides on-site aboard one of these old behemoths.

The museum is run by the Atlanta chapter of the National Railway Historical Society. Each fall it sponsors a series of scenic train rides through parts of north Georgia.

To reach the Southeastern Railway Museum, take I-85 north and exit onto Route 378 (Beaver Ruin Road), turning left over the interstate. Follow that to U.S. 23 (Buford Highway) and turn right. The museum is on the right just past the Duluth city limits. Driving time from Atlanta is about 30 minutes. The museum is open every Saturday year-round from 10 a.m. to 5 p.m. and on Sunday of "steam up" weekends from noon to 5 p.m. Picnic tables are available and the place caters to birthday parties. Admission is $4 for adults and $2 for seniors and kids on "steam up" days; just a $1 charge other times. Telephone: 706/476-2013.

6. The Alexander Stephens Home

On the Path of Duty

IN 1859 Alexander Stephens of Crawfordville finished his eighth term representing an east Georgia district in Congress. He had grown a bit weary of it all and felt he was through with politics. Events soon dragged him back to the path of duty and proved him wrong.

Elected vice president of the Confederacy in 1861, he subsequently served as a commissioner at the peace conference in Virginia and was later imprisoned in Massachusetts. Duty continued to call. From 1873 to 1882 he again served in the House of Representatives, and in 1882 he became governor of Georgia.

Frail physically, Stephens was mighty in mind and spirit. A lawyer and historian, he put the citizenry first. A tour of his Crawfordville home reveals a bit of the individual behind the public man.

Stephens called his home **Liberty Hall**, inspired apparently not from political sentiment but from hospitality. Guests were always welcome, and strangers passing through town were "at liberty" to stay the night. He bought the place in 1845 after graduating from the University of Georgia, briefly teaching school and studying law under Williamson Bird who had owned the house. He made some additions in 1858 and remodeled it in the 1870s. Stephens died in 1883, and the interpretation covers the period from 1875 until his death. The state acquired Liberty Hall in 1932 and completed a $100,000 restoration in 1989.

A spacious lawn rolls up to the broad veranda of the house, dividing at the Stephens monument and grave. A simple but inviting exterior reflects an interior emphasis on comfort and utility. Still, the house can claim touches of class.

In one front corner you find Stephens' bedroom, complete with his desk, bed, wheelchair and medicine bottles. The wallpaper is a faithful copy of the original. Behind the bedroom is a sitting room with sofa, 1870s rolltop desk, small chess table, and another table set for whist. Here you'll begin to note some of the details that make the house a gem; for example, period lace curtains and a green mantel scarf.

Across the hallway (its floor painted in a black and red-brown diamond pattern) is the dining room with another wheelchair and an early 19th-century drop-leaf table resting atop a crumb cloth.

On the southwest corner, the parlor glows with decorative treasures—vases filled with feathers instead of flowers, a shadow box containing human hair, a what-not lined with curios, a mantel scarf, an organ, a sofa bed, and lovely hand-painted window shades.

The upper floor consists of an assortment of bedrooms. There's the "tramps room" with twin beds for passersby who needed lodging or for law students studying with Stephens, his nephew's room and his niece's room. Over Stephens' bedroom is the one he kept ready for his close friend and fellow pol, Robert Toombs, whenever that worthy should visit from nearby Washington, Georgia. You're struck by the magnificent four-poster, positively regal with red canopy and gold tassles. The wallpaper is a soft blue, reportedly both men's favorite color.

Connected to the rear of the house is a wing that housed Stephens' library, a spare bedroom, and a wine cellar beneath. The wing even has its own porch. On the shelves, weighty tomes tend toward history, law and government.

To the side sits the kitchen, separated from the house to reduce heat and the danger of fire. Period items include a mop made of corn sheaves, a butter churn, a cork presser (to seal medicine bottles), candle molds, meat grinders, and a very nice corner cabinet.

Some yards away you find quarters for slaves (servants after the war). A wash house conveniently situated next to a well was reconstructed by the Civilian Conservation Corps in the 1930s.

The site offers a bonus in the form of a small, compact **Confederate Museum** that not only yields details of soldiers' lives but illustrates to a degree what the Georgia homefront was like during the war. You see typical tableware, cooking utensils, sewing and spinning equipment, quilts and linen, and an Emerson grand piano. Then there are quotes from the battlefront—excerpts from letters and diaries—that speak of hardship, fear, patriotism and death. In addition to pikes, sabers and other weapons, the collection comprises mundane items such as hairbrushes, cups, belts, a leather cigar holder, a portable writing desk, a fife, and family portraits in miniature. There's even a stomach-turning account of treating wounds and gangrene. In one display, a couple of Confederate manikins smoke by their tent and evening fire, with captioned quotation that reads, "A soldier's usual occupation has whiled away my time, listening to vulgar songs, yarns...smoking and reading."

At the end of the exhibit, you encounter a particularly poignant portrait—a 1914 photo of white-haired veterans from Taliaferro County—as well as an electoral ticket offering Jefferson Davis of Mississippi as president and Alexander Stephens of Georgia as vice president—a winning, and losing, team. It ended more than 130 years ago, but the War Between the States is never distant in these parts.

The Alexander Stephens Home is a little over one and one-half hours from Atlanta. Take I-20 east to exit 55. Follow Route 22 north and turn east on U.S. 278 to Crawfordville. Go left at Monument Street, then left on Park and right on Alexander. Liberty Hall and the museum are open Tuesday through Saturday 9 a.m. to 5 p.m., Sundays 2 p.m. to 5 p.m.; closed Mondays. Admission is $1.75 for adults, $1 for kids. Telephone: 706/456-2221. (NOTE: The home of Stephens' friend Robert Toombs is in Washington, 21 miles north via Routes 22 and 44, and is also open to visitors.)

7. Tallulah Falls

Taking the Plunge

IN midsummer 1970, high-wire meister Karl Wallenda stepped onto a 1-11/16th-inch-thick steel cable strung across 1,200-foot-deep Tallulah Gorge in northeast Georgia. Why? To get to the other side, of course. Well, also to earn a $10,000 fee and bring a burst of publicity and crowd of spectators to this area that seven decades earlier had been one of the Southeast's prominent resorts. Reportedly, actress Tallulah Bankhead was named after the place.

The stroll took the 67-year-old Wallenda about 16 minutes—he even paused midway for a headstand on the wire. But the stunt didn't draw tourists much after that. Today, a new state park and the promise of occasional whitewater in the gorge may in the long run do a better job than Wallenda.

At the turn of the century the town of Tallulah Falls counted at least a dozen hotels plus a railroad that carted in honeymooners and vacationers. The main attraction was the Tallulah River's thundering falls, called by some "the Niagara of the South." The gorge drops 600 feet in two miles where the river has cut its way through ancient quartzite. But Georgia Power Company dammed the river in 1913 for hydroelectricity, effectively turning off the tap. That dried up the tourist trade.

Eighty years later, conservationists and recreation types sought at least occasional releases of water over the cliffs for scenic beauty and some full-bore kayaking. The Federal Energy Regulatory Commission seemed to agree, and Georgia Power, to get its hydro operation re-licensed, proposed a modest constant flow and a several-times yearly heavy cascade. Meanwhile, the state has leased 3,000 acres from the utility to create a park around the gorge. The vicinity just behind the dam will have a visitors center and interpretive museum, the latter taking visitors back through time from today's hydro power to the golden resort era to the area's natural history. You will find picnic tables, tennis courts and campsites, plus areas for swimming and canoeing. Plans call for a trail along part of the north rim connecting to a south-rim trail via a bridge across the chasm. Georgia's Department of Natural Resources may designate rock-climbing zones in the gorge.

Even before the completion of the new complex, a visit to the area shows Tallulah's promise and its past.

It seems just another roadside attraction as you approach from the south and swing off the main road toward the canyon's edge. You pass the touristy Indian Spring Trading Post and arrive at a string of faded souvenir and antique shops punctuated by a small-scale Statue of Liberty holding aloft a glass globe. Signs direct you to "see where Wallenda walked the wire."

On the other side, along the north rim, you find toppled steel rusting among the pines, rhododendron and holly. There's no legend on it but it matches a construction across the gorge, a relic of Wallenda's gig. The view from here is grand, and better still with the water on.

Going upstream from the Terrora visitors center building, you'll find the relocated old Tallulah jail, additional hiking trails and the remains of a railroad trestle. The Tallulah Falls Railroad, or "old TF," reached the town in 1882 and was the end of the line for a couple of decades before the route pushed on to North Carolina. Some 42 trestles once carried 58 miles of track over streams and along the gorge.

Lake Rabun, **Lake Burton** and **Panther Creek** are among nearby scenic spots, and a drive to **Glen-Ella Springs**, a 100-year-old three-story inn, gives a glimpse of the rustic charm that helped make the area so popular a century ago.

To reach Tallulah Falls, take I-85 north and exit onto I-985. Pick up U.S. 23 and U.S. 441 northeast out of Gainesville and follow that road right to the town. Travel time from Atlanta is about one hour and 30

TALLULAH FALLS

minutes. Expect a nominal fee for parking or admission to the museum. The park, open seven days, has normal hours roughly equivalent to available daylight. Telephone: 706/754-8257.

8. Georgia's Wine Country

Fruit of the Vine

JOT this down for your trivia file—Georgia is the country's fifth-largest wine-producing state, after California, New York, Washington, and South Carolina, at least according to one wine industry source. Although winemaking in Georgia dates back to James Oglethorpe's first settlement, the modern era of the grape began as recently as the early 1980s.

Georgia's wine country bears little resemblance to Bordeaux, the Moselle or the Napa Valley, but an afternoon at three different wineries northeast of Atlanta reveals how firmly the vines have taken root here. (In fairness, it should be noted that a budding vineyard called Fox Winery exists southeast of Atlanta in Social Circle.)

The first stop is **Chestnut Mountain** winery in Braselton, about 45 minutes up I-85. Established in 1988, it's pretty much a two-man operation but both owners studied winemaking in California and know how to produce a decent cabernet.

A faux castle houses the modest operation—2,500 cases annually—standing in a meadow surrounded by forest and fronted by a small vineyard the fruit of which goes to home winemakers. Most of the winery's grapes come from vineyards near Commerce.

Inside you'll find a small tasting counter and a gift rack, the latter selling T-shirts, caps, bottleholders, corkscrews and such. The owners will gladly answer questions and give a 15- to 20-minute tour, pointing out fermenting casks, pressing gear and the small bottling line where the stockholders, they say, occasionally assist with bottling and with quality assurance. It's very informal and informative.

Chestnut Mountain produces a cabernet sauvignon, a chardonnay and a red table wine called Phoenix. The company hopes to expand its line to include a blush and a white under the

Phoenix label and perhaps a sauvignon blanc. It also plans to expand the facility itself, gradually adding space for greater production and for a banquet/tasting room. Visiting hours (good idea to call first) are Tuesday through Saturday 10 a.m. to 6 p.m., Sundays 12:30 p.m. to 6 p.m., closed Mondays. The winery hosts festivals in April and October.

About a mile west and across I-85 stands 2,400-acre **Chateau Elan**, playing Cadillac to Chestnut Mountain's Miata. The largest Georgia winery, Chateau Elan is as much resort as grape grinder, containing a pricey restaurant, spa, golf course, and equestrian center. The main building resembles a 16th-century French chateau. Still, it hasn't forgotten its origins. It plants 200 acres, and tours and tastings are offered Monday through Saturday (hourly) 11 a.m. to 5 p.m. and Sundays 12:30 p.m. to 5 p.m. Once a month for a $5 fee you can take a "meet the winemaker" tour.

On regular tours you first view a mural which, in Rabelasian-like strokes, illustrates the 5,000-year history of winemaking, then watch a video that discusses growing and harvesting of grapes, pressing, fermenting, storage and bottling, as well as the development of Chateau Elan which planted its first vines in 1983.

The tour then moves to the two-story pressing/fermenting room where you encounter more than 20 towering tanks and the pressing equipment. It's then downstairs to the cask room with its racks of oak barrels. Here you can look in on the bottling and labeling room. The bottling line at Chateau Elan is perhaps five times bigger than the one at Chestnut Mountain. The guide explains the shapes, colors and traditions of wine bottles.

Back upstairs in the tasting room, your guide will give you a lesson in wine tasting, employing the French *tastevin*—a shallow, silver, pock-marked cup. Visitors sample four to six varieties of Chateau Elan's 15 labels, ranging from riesling to merlot and including one of its specialty muscadine wines. An extensive gift shop sells wines and wine-related items. Events are held monthly, and the place offers a summer music fest as well.

Less than an hour north is **Habersham Winery** in Baldwin. The company has several tasting rooms/gift shops throughout north Georgia; however, this is the site of wine production (with a more recent one in Helen, Georgia). Tours of the winery are available on request, but it's a good idea to call first, and the "action" occurs between late August and early October during harvest. The winery is open to the public Monday through Saturday 10 a.m. to 6 p.m., Sundays 1 p.m. to 6 p.m.

Like Chestnut Mountain, Habersham gets most of its grapes from off-site vineyards, in this case near Clarkesville. Production began in 1983 and reached 2,000 cases, a figure that rose to 10,000 a decade later.

In 1994 Habersham introduced its Creekstone label, a line of premium wines more akin in body and flavor to the Californians. There's a modest charge to taste these (chardonnay, pinot noir, merlot, and cabernet franc); sampling the others is free.

At the gift shop/tasting room, you not only find the usual T-shirts, corkscrews and such, but also books on growing grapes and paraphernalia for making your own wine.

To reach Chestnut Mountain and Chatau Elan, take I-85 north and get off at exit 48 (east for the former and turn right at the stop sign; and west for the latter—you can't miss it). For Habersham, take exit 50 off I-85 and follow U.S. 129 toward Gainesville, then proceed north on I-985 which becomes Route 365/U.S. 23 into Baldwin (the place is on the left near mile marker 41). Travel time from Chateau Elan to Habersham is about 50 minutes. For more information about these three wineries, call 770/867-6914 for Chestnut Mountain, 800/233-9463 for Chateau Elan, and 706/778-9463 for Habersham.

9. The Bill Elliott Racing Museum

Life in the Fast Lane

THEY call him "Awesome Bill from Dawsonville," and you can file his biography under the heading: Hometown boy makes good—fast!

NASCAR superstar Bill Elliott hails from Dawsonville, about an hour north of Atlanta, and if you enjoy auto racing you might want to cruise on up to this museum/souvenir center that also serves as headquarters of the Bill Elliott Fan Club. Photos, trophies, mementos, and lean, mean machines testify to this driver's achievements and popularity.

The small lobby displays family photos, official proclamations and shots of Elliott in action. In the main hall, one set of cases contains such items as 1974 trophies from Dixie Speedway; red and white coveralls emblazoned with patches marked Melling, Motorcraft, Camel, Ford, and IROC; a coverlet with his Number 9 Ford sewn on it; trophies from Pocono, Daytona and Budweiser 500s; a mounted chunk of tire from the 1992 "March Madnes" races at Rockingham, Richmond, Atlanta and Darlington; and pole award plaques from the 1993 Winston Cup Series.

A 45-minute video, *Bill Elliott—Racing into History*, introduces visitors to the man, his machines, his supporting cast, and his winning ways.

Numerous wall photos show Winston Cup drivers, racing scenes and finish-line poses. One prominent picture records Elliott receiving a $1 million check as winner of the "Winston Million" in 1985.

Then there are the cars—the 1985 Thunderbird that won the Winston Cup, a 1937 Ford convertible roadster and a 1971 Boss 351 Mustang both owned by Elliott, and the T-bird winner of the 1987 Daytona 500. A closeup look at one Number 9 shows the stripped-down interior, the simplified dash and special gauges, the protective bars and braces; not many comfort options in these babies. A neaby exhibit shows front and rear wheel racing assemblies.

Demonstrating and appreciating fan support is part of the museum's goal. Display cases hold letters, photos, mementos and illustrations, ranging from crayon drawings to Christmas cards to Coors-can ships. There are objects you'd expect to see—such as model cars and auto racing collector cards—and articles you wouldn't: for example, a canoe paddle from Canada and a rock from Saudi Arabia collected during Operation Desert Storm. And caps, "gimmie caps" from across the country—Johnson Ford in Spearfish, South Dakota; Southern Railway Builders; Planet Hollywood; and Papa's Pizza to Go.

Some folks have set their sentiments to verse. Ensconced on one shelf is an engraved 14-stanza poem entitled, "Man from Dawsonville," and on the far wall hangs another poetic tribute, "A Real Winner," in which the author notes, "He's the fastest driver on the NASCAR track/Before the rest get started...Bill's already back."

There's a gold-plated hammer from Tru-Value given to Elliott for being a "Hard Charger" as well as a "collector's edition" of wrenches from Snap-On Tools. And he's not forgotten by his neighbors. The inscription on one tall trophy reads, "Thanks Bill Elliott and the Melling Race Team for Bringing Honor and National Attention to Dawson County, Georgia." No question about it.

Also on hand are lots of T-shirts, key rings, cups, mugs, posters, caps, *NASCAR Legend* comics, and other souvenirs for sale.

If auto racing is your thing, you're less than an hour from where the engines roar and the rubber meets the track. Take Route 53 east from Dawsonville and past Gainesville to I-85. Within a few miles or exits of one another, you'll find **Atlanta Dragway**, a quarter-mile stretch for high-powered sprint cars; **Lanier Raceway**, a three-eighths-mile stock car track billed as part of the Winston Cup series; and **Road Atlanta**, a two-and-a-half-mile course for sports cars, go-karts and motorcycles where actor Paul Newman once raced.

THE BILL ELLIOTT RACING MUSEUM

To reach the Bill Elliott Racing Museum, take Route 400 (a toll road) north to Route 53 and proceed west on it straight through Dawsonville. A few miles outside of town, bear right on Route 183; the place is a couple of miles up on the left. Driving time from Atlanta is about an hour. Admission is free. The facility is open Monday through Saturday 9:30 a.m. to 4:30 p.m., closed Sundays. Telephone: 706/265-2718. (NOTE: To obtain information on activities at the above tracks, call 706/335-2301 for Atlanta Dragway, 770/967-2131 for Lanier Raceway, and 770/967-6143 for Road Atlanta.)

10. The Commerce Connection

Shop Till You Drop

SO you like a bargain, love to shop, have some space in the suitcase or trunk? Or maybe you own a researcher's interest in American consumerism? Whatever, you might consider visiting the aptly named city of Commerce.

You get a hint of what's to come along the interstate just outside the perimeter highway when you notice the Georgia Antiques Center, Dinette Warehouse, Marble Outlet, Golf Warehouse, and furniture and carpet outlets, even one for swimming pools and saunas. But farther up I-85 just before exit 53, you see a billboard for the real thing.

The **Tanger Outlet Mall** just off the interstate plays to that old adage, "When the going gets tough, the tough go shopping." Nearly four dozen stores on several acres of sun-baked asphalt enable you to purchase almost anything except nuclear weapons, and all at cut-rate prices.

Most of the shops take plastic, but if you need cash there's an automatic teller machine on-site. And lest you think the North Carolina-based mangement of Tanger doesn't care about its customers, behold the suggestion box conveniently placed on the wall of the mall. Near the restrooms (complete with diaper-changing tables) is a customer lounge. And outside in the hallway you encounter a mural billed as a museum—667 square feet of acrylic and latex panels depicting local history painted by a self-trained artist.

But you're here to shop, not relax. So check it out. Clothes? They got clothes. Carter's Outlet and Oshkosh B'gosh cover the kiddies, infant to size 10. Women's undergarments and sleepwear fill Barbizon and Maidenform, with many items at excellent prices. Woolrich offers men's and women's sportswear, outdoor wear and blankets, some up to 50 percent off retail. Try Bannister for name-brand shoes at up to 70 percent off. At Liz Claiborne you must hunt down the deals, but damaged articles are labeled such and run half price. Bugle Boy outfits the teenagers; no seconds here. And no jean-splicing at Levi's. Cape Isle Knitters sells nice-looking women's vests, sweaters and jerseys advertised at 25 percent to 50 percent off every day. The Reebok store carries a variety of athletic shoes at around $13 to $17 off list prices.

Something for setting the table? Lenox China features selected seconds, overstock, special items and discontinued pieces at reduced prices. Dansk serves up fashionable, contemporary dinnerware. And at Oneida you can find various crystal patterns at $8 to $15 off retail, plus candleholders and coffee/tea sets marked down nearly 50 percent and sterling silver at half price.

If this works up an appetite, you might pop into the Sara Lee shop for some discount calories in the form of layer cakes, cheesecakes, muffins, and croissants.

Black & Decker sells all sorts of hardware—from power screwdrivers to cordless mowers—at reduced prices. Several stores market wallets, purses, backpacks and bags. Dan River specializes in linens and Corning/Revere in housewares. There are even shops devoted solely to socks, toys, ribbons, cosmetics, and fudge.

But wait! There's more! Across the street beckon the **Commerce Factory Stores**—Izod, Boston Trader, Arrow, Gold Toe, Book Warehouse, and others waiting to feed your shopping need.

Over here, too, you find a Texas-size bazaar with a touch of Tijuana called **The Pottery**. If you enter through the garden section, which markets all manner of exotic and traditional plants, you pull up short at the rim of "The Canyon." Sure enough, you peer into a chasm of plants, ranging from azaleas to junipers. Banks and beds and pathways line the steep sides and a small mill wheel turns in the stream bed at the bottom. The entire "Pottery Plant" counts some 30 greenhouses and covers 25 acres, with plans to add a 75-acre shrub and tree farm.

Across The Canyon, merchandise mounts up in this supply depot for America's back yard—aluminum windchimes and ceramic birdhouses, ranks of painted lamp posts and piles of white bird cages, scores of cloned gargoyle wall sconces and leonine lavabos. You'll see myriad terracotta planters, some big enough to bury a body in, but nicely priced. Beyond rest dozens of straight-back metallic garden chairs lined up as for a lecture. Some tags showed a four-foot-high windmill going for $44, a squat-winged gargoyle for $24, and a six-foot-tall Statue of Liberty for $802. A few bucks will buy you some petite terracotta feet. You also see rough-hewn fountain bowls, sundry religious statuary and concrete ducks assaulting a dwarf. Stated policy says, "Our mistake, your gain—half price."

Back inside are rooms and aisles and counters—over 150,000 square feet—of wicker, plaster, wrought iron, brass; of Christmas and Halloween items; of silk and dried flowers; of dishes, mugs and glasses; of Mexico products and more. It's an experience, if not a sale.

Commerce wasn't always like this. Once named Harmony Grove, it served as the model for the bucolic turn-of-the-century town of Cold Sassy in Olive Ann Burns' *Cold Sassy Tree*. How things change.

Commerce's "outlet city" is about an hour northeast of Atlanta just off I-85. (Another Tanger Outlet Mall has opened on I-75 between Atlanta and Macon.) Open all year Monday through Saturday 9 a.m. to 9 p.m., Sundays noon to 6 p.m. Neighboring emporia have similar hours. Free admission. Telephone: 706/335-4537.

11. Butts-Mehre Heritage Hall

How 'Bout Them Dawgs!

FOOTBALL frenzy forms an integral part of autumn life in Georgia and nowhere more so than in Athens, home of the University of Georgia Bulldogs. Georgia football seems equal parts tradition, pride, loyalty and identity. It even rates a plug in that rockin' tune, "Come Together." And you know you're approaching the campus when you spot a billboard showing a player about to pitch the pigskin, accompanied by the caption: "Bulldog Spirit—Pass It On."

That spirit has its own dog house, if you will, a veritable shrine to the school's athletic prowess called Butts-Mehre Heritage Hall. Named for football coaches Wally Butts (1939- 1960) and Harry Mehre (1928-1937) and opened in 1987, the stunning 78,000-square-foot structure is made of black glass and red granite. Overlooking the track venue and practice football field, it houses the university's pantheon of heroes, such as football greats Frank Sinkwich, Charley Trippi, Fran Tarkenton and Herschel Walker, but it sings the praises of other sports, too. And it's not solely a showcase—numerous athletics-related offices are located here as well as training facilities and locker rooms.

The heart of the hall, from a heritage standpoint, is the third-floor exhibit area, easily accessible via the main entrance. The display cases, containing athletic artifacts from several decades, resemble one another, so you must search and sample. All told, the hall holds 20 cubicles and ten color transparency displays. Four video kiosks let you relive great moments in University of Georgia sports history. And there are the trophies—one from the 1984 Cotton Bowl where Georgia beat Texas, 10-9, and one for the 1980 national championship, among many others.

The cubicle cases contain all manner of memorabilia marking both Georgia's and America's sports past. There's a piece of the wooden goalpost dismembered after Georgia beat Yale, 26-7, in 1931; a 1901 baseball glove; Frank Sinkwich's helmet and the protective chin guard he wore when he played with a broken jaw in 1941. One exhibit shows the development of football helmets from leather flattops to today's well-padded composite models. You meet the 1990 national champs in baseball and the 1985 and 1987 national tennis champs. The hall offers everything from women's basketball to the evolution of Uga, the famed bulldog who adorns T-shirts, caps and bumperstickers (this last with the line, "Let the Big Dawg Eat!"). There are cases, too, on Coach (and later Athletic Director) Vince Dooley and premier running back Herschel Walker. Women get their due as well; for example, basketball heroine Theresa Edwards and track star Gwen Torrence played here.

You learn football came to Athens in 1891 courtesy of Dr. Charles Herty who arranged a game between Georgia and Mercer, the first football game in the Deep South. Glenn "Pop" Warner, Georgia's first paid coach, went on to renown at Carlisle. Football here really took hold in 1929 when Georgia beat powerhouse Yale, 15-0. Frank Sinkwich was the first Bulldog to win the Heisman Trophy, named for Coach John Heisman of archrival Georgia Tech.

The fourth floor fans fan interest too, presenting old uniforms, programs, records and photos. You reach this floor by elevator, the buttons of which are labeled "Hunker up" and "Hunker down," an apparent reference to Bulldog followers' plea when the going gets tough: "Hunker down, you hairy dawgs!"

Athens is about 65 miles northeast of Atlanta via U.S. 78. Travel time to the University of Georgia campus runs an hour and a quarter to an hour and a half, depending on traffic. Butts-Mehre Heritage Hall, on the corner of Pinecrest and Rutherford, is open Monday through Friday 8 a.m. to 5 p.m., Saturdays and Sundays 2 p.m. to 5 p.m. Admission is free. Telephone: 706/542-9094.

Northeast Quadrant

Here and There

THE highways and byways of northeast Georgia offer splendid opportunities for rubbernecking and relaxation. For example, in **Clermont** on Route 129 and along Route 400 toward Dahlonega you may see whole herds of artificial animals. All of downtown **Helen** is ersatz Bavarian and the upper **Chatthoochee River** here is popular for tubing.

At **Lake Lanier**, one of the nation's most heavily used Corps of Engineers lakes and venue for rowing in the 1996 Olympics, you can swim, picnic and rent boats. In nearby Gainesville, the Green Street Station displays the **Mark Trail Memorabilia Exhibit**, personal collection of illustrator Ed Dodd who originated the *Mark Trail* comic strip.

The **Navy Supply Corps Museum** in Athens tells the 200-year history of that branch via ship models, navigational gear, paintings and memorabilia. Athens also is home to the **Georgia State Botanical Garden**.

In **Madison**, just north of I-20 and an hour east of Atlanta, you can drive through "the town that Sherman spared" and feast your eyes on beautiful antebellum and Victorian homes.

Closer to the city, in Loganville, the **Vines Botanical Garden** covers 25 acres of greenery, floral beds, pathways, fountains and trees.

Up in the Sautee Valley near Cleveland and Helen, you'll find a plethora of pottery at **Mark of the Potter**. Cleveland itself is home to Babyland General where **Cabbage Patch Kids** are "born."

If your musical taste turns to banjos and fiddles, don't miss the **Bluegrass Festiva**l in Dahlonega each June. And for more on rural life and history take in the summertime **Georgia Mountain Fair** in Hiawasee and "The Reach of Song," a dramatic presentation based on the life and works of poet Byron Herbert Reece. For Old World style goings-on in the New, head for Helen's **Oktoberfest**.

Southeast of Atlanta

SOUTHEAST OF ATLANTA

(1) Andersonville
(2) Piedmont National Wildlife Refuge
(3) Jarrell Plantation
(4) The Hay House
(5) Eatonton
(6) The Museum of Aviation
(7) Ocmulgee National Monument
(8) Milledgeville
(9) Panola Mountain

1. Andersonville

Portrait of POWs

SOME two hours south of Atlanta in a quiet little corner of Georgia you will find a unique historic spot, a patch of ground that is more than cemetery—although it is one—and more than museum—but that also is here—and more than memorial—again, part of the picture. It's a place that forms an indelible image in our collective conscience, a collage of fear, hope, shame, misfortune, courage and despair. It is Andersonville, former Confederate prisoner of war camp and now a National Historic Site.

Today you might catch the smell of new-mown grass, perhaps a whiff of piney woods. You might see a handful of visitors strolling by trees, monuments and a modest creek. Had you been unlucky enough to have been here in late 1864 you would have witnessed 30,000 men crammed into 27 acres, sick with scurvy, dysentery and gangrene, beset by flies and mosquitoes, existing in handmade shelters near an open sewer.

As one inmate wrote, "One-third of the original enclosure was swampy—a mud of liquid filth, voidings from the thousands, seething with maggots in full activity. We could not get away from it—we ate it, drank it and slept in it."

Officially known as Camp Sumter, Andersonville was chosen as a POW site when it became evident the war would not end quickly and facilities around Richmond were full. The prisoner exchange system had faltered, and a remote, secure place at the end of a railroad line would better serve. Originally designed to hold 6,000 men, it was surrounded by a pine-log stockade with guard towers or "pigeon roosts" every 30 yards. The dead were placed in a mass grave outside the prison, and clothing was so precious many bodies were buried naked.

The visitors center introduces you to the rigors and routine of

POW life—scavenging, bartering, working burial details, digging wells (and escape tunnels), mending clothes, keeping diaries. Artifacts include some of those diaries, a carved cane and pipe bowl, part of the original gate, a map of the camp drawn from memory, a key to the gate, a homemade mending kit called a "housewife." And there are the young men in the photos: the "faces of Andersonville," with a note inviting visitors to submit pictures of POWs or guards their families may yet possess.

(You learn, too, that Andersonville and other Confederate POW camps in North Carolina and Virginia had no monopoly on suffering. The Union had similar facilities in New York, Maryland, Ohio, Indiana, and Illinois, and although conditions were generally better in the North thousands died there as well.)

Those shown are the "before" shots, individual soldiers prior to battle, prior to capture. Photos of emaciated Union POWs were published in *Harper's Weekly*, generating outrage in the North and cries for revenge. A war crimes trial found stockade commandant Captain Henry Wirz guilty and sentenced him to hang.

The site now is a cemetery for soliders of all wars, but perhaps the most sobering stretch runs between the visitors center and the stockade site where the roadway passes between two sections of Andersonville's original dead. Row after row of small, white headstones stand side by side, etched with name, state and ID number, the uniform ranks broken only by a sheltering oak or fir or by a state-donated monument.

At the prison site itself, green, clipped grass covers the awful ground. Markers outline the stockade wall and the so-called "dead-line" which prisoners were forbidden to cross. Replicas of sections of the stockade, punishment racks and various crude shelters bring the setting out of the abstract. You'll see the same sluggish stream that served as laundry and toilet, and on the west side Providence Spring, which beautifully bubbled forth at the height of the misery.

Andersonville's contemporary purpose involves telling America's entire POW story, not only that chapter of the Civil War. Accordingly, the **National Prisoner of War Museum** houses information and exhibits dating back to the American Revolution and including the Persian Gulf War. Emphasis is on World War II; any notion that *Hogan's Heroes* realistically depicted the situation quickly vanishes. There are materials relating to the actual "Great Escape," photos of the Bataan Death March, an exhibit of how the POW "grapevine" worked in a German *stalag*. The segment on Korea outlines the harsh conditions made worse by political indoctrination. From the Vietnam War comes a diagram of the infamous "Hanoi Hilton."

The museum provides a display of historic contrasts, too: 400,000 German POWs, 50,000 Italians and 5,000 Japanese were imprisoned in the United States during World War II. Some 12,000 occupied 34 camps in Georgia where they farmed, forested, played soccer, and even took college courses.

Andersonville National Historic Site is about two hours and 15 minutes south of Atlanta. Take I-75 south to exit 46 at Byron. Go south on Route 49, also called Peach Parkway and POW Trail, through Fort Valley, Marshallville, Montezuma and Oglethorpe. Admission is free, but donations are welcome. The site is open daily 8 a.m. to 5 p.m. Telephone: 912/924-0343.

2. Piedmont National Wildlife Refuge

More than an Animal Shelter

IN area, Georgia is the largest state east of the Mississippi River and it remains a rural state in many respects. But that doesn't mean it's a home where the buffalo or any other animals may freely and safely roam. Nearly everywhere, wildlife needs a sanctuary, and in middle Georgia they can find it at the Piedmont National Wildlife Refuge, north of Macon.

Covering 35,000 acres, the refuge was established in 1939 as part of a federal program demonstrating that unproductive acreage could be reclaimed to restore the land and provide habitat for wild animals. More than a century of plantation farming had removed the trees and depleted the land. By 1880 no virgin forest remained. Topsoil disappeared in the rain and floods. The boll weevil decimated the cotton crop. By the mid-1930s people were abandoning their farms.

The concept of the refuge was, in part, to let nature rejuvenate the exhausted landscape, with a little human assistance. Today this revitalized patch of earth is home to wild turkeys, deer, flying squirrels, rabbits, foxes, snakes, bobcats, raccoons, possums, coyotes, hawks, salamanders, owls, the endangered red-cockaded woodpecker and many other species.

A visit to the refuge enables you to examine this protected environment in various ways. The visitors center houses exhibits concerning the area's flora and fauna. On the back deck hangs a hummingbird feeder which attracts the tiny whirr-wings. And on the ground is a small rock pool just right for tadpoles and frogs.

Some display cases have earphones so that you can listen to a short description or explanation of the habitat on view, for instance a beaver dam. And wall-mounted photos and text recount how and why the refuge was built.

Numerous trees stock the restored landscape, and another

display here shows the diverse trunks side by side, permitting identification by bark color and texture—water oak, sweet gum, black cherry, dogwood, loblolly pine, and more.

A more interactive exhibit is a sandbox to which cords connect small wooden blocks. The bottoms of the blocks are embossed with replicas of animals' feet so that you can make prints in the sand and recognize the tracks, be they blue heron, cottontail rabbit or other critter.

The refuge has a six-mile wildlife drive, a gravel road with numbered stops corresponding to entries in a leaflet that describes habitats and other features of the course, including refuge management programs and practices.

There are a couple of hiking trails, too—a one-mile route around **Allison Lake** and a three-mile trek that goes near a colony of red-cockaded woodpeckers. The former may reveal beaver or otter, wood ducks or kingfishers and, if you're lucky, an eagle. An old moonshine still testifies to an earlier human presence here. The second trail winds through different types of terrain, from open woodland to creekside bottomland. You may see herons, hawks, tiny toads, animal tracks and lovely wildflowers. But be

PIEDMONT NATIONAL WILDLIFE REFUGE

advised: this is tick territory. Long pants, a potent repellent and a sharp-eyed post-hike check are highly recommended. In summer it's also hot and humid; you'll be glad you packed a canteen.

Piedmont National Wildlife Refuge, located a few miles from **Jarrell Plantation**, *is about one hour and 25 minutes from Atlanta. Take I-75 south and get off at exit 61. Go east on Route 18 through Juliette and follow the signs. Admission is free. The refuge is open Monday through Friday 8 a.m. to 4:30 p.m., Saturdays and Sundays 9 a.m. to 5:30 p.m.; closed on federal holidays. Telephone: 912/986-5441.*

3. Jarrell Plantation

Down to Earth

THE term "plantation" may elicit images of stately, white-pillared elegance and stereotypical Old South lifestyles, but there's nothing romantic, rich or refined about Jarrell Plantation north of Macon. This family spread, dating back to the 1840s, reflects hard work, ingenuity and self-sufficiency.

Founded by John Fitz Jarrell and expanded by his son Dick in the early 1900s, the place embraced 600 acres and claimed nearly 40 slaves by the beginning of the Civil War. Jarrell was one of Georgia's 3,600 plantation farmers, mainstays then of the state's economy. Union troops raided the place and burned its cotton gin, but within a decade John Jarrell had regained a measure of prosperity.

Dick Jarrell put in a grist mill and a sawmill, farmed 360 acres and turned the place into a quite a factory—grinding cornmeal, sawing timber, ginning cotton and making cane syrup for neighboring plantations. In 1974 a descendant donated seven and one-half acres, including the old buildings and implements, to the state for historical purposes. Some 90 percent of the artifacts are original Jarrell possessions, making this one of the largest family collections in Georgia.

You enter through a visitors center which displays farm gear and early appliances as well as cotton bolls and family photos. It also offers a seven-minute slide show recounting the plantation's history.

A self-guided tour passes first by the traditional garden which bears the same sort of crops the Jarrells raised here a century or more ago—corn, beans, squash, cabbage, sugar cane, and cotton. You then see a chicken coop, a metal-roofed barn, a three-hole privy, and a shed where salt-cured meats were hung.

On the left you'll encounter Dick's first house, a slant-roof

JARRELL PLANTATION

Cotton Gin, Jarrell Plantation

frame structure with two bedrooms in front containing crib, beds, desk and mirror-dresser. Farther along the path you come across kettles used for washing clothes and an outdoor furnace with two large cast-iron cisterns used for making syrup, rendering lard and scalding hog hides. The family wasn't much into imports; they tanned their own leather, made their own clothes from cotton and flax, and fashioned their own furniture, looms and spinning wheels.

At the top of the hill sits John's house, a modest frame dwelling holding handmade hunt board, cradle, looms and chairs. Standing against the walls are a pair of hand-fashioned crutches and a long stick with fabric strips called a shoo-fly. Feather beds have their original handmade coverlets. One room in the house served as a store in the early 1900s, selling sausage, walnuts, candy, syrup, pins, and other items. Well-informed site attendants will tell you the benefits of elevating the house a foot and one-half off the ground and explain why most structures lack paint; indeed, they'll have the answer for almost any question you pose.

A path winding down the hill leads you to the various family-constructed work sheds where you see a steam engine, circular saw blades, cotton gin and evaporating room, all part of Dick Jarrell's mill complex. The 1909 wood-burning steam boiler and steam engine are original equipment, too. Also on hand is a 500-pound bale of cotton.

Other buildings completing this early agribusiness portrait consist of an equipment shed, blacksmith shop and wheat house, the latter hung with boiler flues serving as counterweights to their rooftop doors which let in sunlight to keep the grain mold-free.

This state historic site hosts several special events during the year, such as a display of 100 years of Jarrell family clothing, sheep-shearing to making shawls, family farm day, a Civil War encampment, and syrup-making and storytelling.

Jarrell Plantation is approximately one hour and 20 minutes from Atlanta. Take I-75 south to exit 61. Go east on Route 18 through the small town of Juliette and across the Ocmulgee River. The road eventually forks left toward Piedmont National Wildlife Refuge and right toward Jarrell Plantation. Admission is $2 for adults, $1 for kids. Normal hours are Tuesday through Saturday 9 a.m. to 5 p.m., Sundays 2 p.m. to 5:30 p.m.; closed on Monday. Telephone: 912/986-5172.

4. The Hay House

History in the Makin'

IN Macon, Georgia in the 1850s homes of the well-to-do tended to follow the Greek Revival style so popular in the antebellum South. This was as true in the Mulberry Street neighborhood near Mercer College as elsewhere in the city. So the mansion of William Butler Johnson, done in Italian Renaissance Revival, stood out. And despite some changes over the years, it still does.

Johnson, a jeweler, had made enough money by age 42 that he could retire. In 1851 he married a woman 20 years his junior and they went abroad, which in those days meant Europe. They traveled, sojourned, had a child, purchased art, appreciated architecture, and hobnobbed with the rich and famous.

They returned to Macon and built their fabulous townhouse, characterized by curves, arches, symmetry and a towering cupola. Also, in contrast to its neighbors, it had walk-in closets, gas lighting, an indoor kitchen with slate floor, hot and cold running water, and a speaker-tube intercom for communicating between rooms and floors. It also boasted a ventilation system consisting of a brick breeze wall to "catch" cool air and a vent tunnel near the root cellar to "store" cool air, which was given entry to the house via shutters in a lower-level door. Double-sash windows let warmer air out at the top and cooler air in at the bottom.

Constructing and furnishing it in that era cost $100,000. In 1926 insurance magnate Parks Lee Hay bought it for $61,500. His heirs gave it to the Georgia Trust for Historical Preservation in 1977.

The exterior originally was scored in stucco to make it resemble large blocks of stone, later replaced by red brick. At the top of the front stairs lies a double circle of stone in the center of which is a quartz cylinder that lets the proper amount of light into the wine cellar below.

To enter you ease past 12-foot-high heart pine doors weighing 500 pounds and swinging softly on sterling silver hinges and ball bearings. Bronze paint imparts a metallic sheen to the massive doors.

The walls in the front hallway were "marbleized" (painted plaster) in a *tromp d'oeil* design to give a three-dimensional stone-finish look. Woodwork in the rear hallway follows this faux 3-D design.

Special touches are everywhere. Some $2,000 in gold leaf decorates an elaborate ceiling in the entranceway. Two pair of curved arched pocket doors slide open and close on sterling silver tracks, reportedly the only such doors in the country. The dining room has an ornate ceiling, a recessed and arched stained-glass window called "Four Seasons of the Vineyard," and an exquisite dark oak mantel entitled "The Hunt." The ballroom—later changed by Johnson's daughter Mary Ellen into a double parlor—is characterized by polychromatic walls and ceiling and by intricate plaster-of-paris molding. Shutters on the tall windows in this room fold back into the wall to allow full light.

The Johnsons included an art gallery to display their acquisitions. Clerestory windows permit natural light and the grained pine paneling cleverly imitates oak. Here you see a unique marble statue of the biblical Ruth by Randolph Rogers—it rotates on a ball-bearing-equipped pedestal. One theory for this feature is that the owners could easily turn the statue away from visitors who might be offended by a bare breast.

The stairway to the next floor is illuminated by an immense stained-glass window in the top of which is set a glass portrait of English poet Lord Byron. The original glass is still luminous with color but the replacement glass has faded, illustrating yet again that they don't make 'em like they used to.

On the landing your tour guide shows you a recess in the wall that has the makings of a mystery. What you discover is more prosaic, but it's a neat turn just the same.

The tour takes you through the family bedrooms, but in summer the residents spent most of their time in the basement level to escape the heat. Part of the living area here was used by Mary

Ellen's husband, Judge Fenton, as a law office and a classroom for his Mercer law students. Down here, too, you see the mansion's larder with its suspended bins and ceiling-based drying racks to foil rats. Beyond are the root and wine cellars and a dungeon-like vent tunnel.

This "Palace of the South" is prime territory for restoration junkies. Guides not only explain evolution of the interior through three generations and families, but also point out swatches of paint or paper denoting particular wall coverings from different years or eras. Even the gift shop joins in—a book rack offers volumes on building rehabilitation/restoration with titles on floor coverings, walls, moldings, and interior decor, plus several books about Victorian homes.

In addition, this is a great place from which to launch further architectural explorations in Macon; for example, the "**Cannonball House**," the **Sidney Lanier Cottage**, the **Woodruff House** and **St. Joseph's Catholic Church**.

To reach the Hay House, take I-75 south and branch off on I-16 at Macon. Take exit 4 onto MLK Drive and cross the Otis Redding Memorial Bridge into town. Turn right on Mulberry and drive up the hill; the mansion is on the left just before the Mercer campus. Driving time from Atlanta is about one hour and 25 minutes. Admission is $6 for adults and $3 for kids. The Hay House is open Monday through Saturday 10 a.m. to 5 p.m., Sundays 1 p.m. to 5 p.m.; closed holidays. Telephone: 912/742-8155.

5. Eatonton

A Rabbit Runs Through It

MANY communities in the South have a statue of a Confederate soldier, poignant and proud, standing near the heart of town. Eatonton, Georgia, claims one too, but unlike its neighbors it also boasts the likeness of a rabbit on the courthouse lawn.

However, this is not any old hare—rather, it's Brer Rabbit, chief character of the Uncle Remus tales and arguably as renowned as White or Peter Rabbit and Bugs or Energizer Bunny. Eatonton is the birthplace, if you will, of Brer Rabbit, Brer Fox, Brer Bear, and the dozens of other critters created by Joel Chandler Harris, for this is where the writer got his start. And just south of the courthouse on the **Antebellum Trail** sits a small museum which tells that story and more.

The **Uncle Remus Museum** building, which opened in 1963, was constructed from slave cabins found in surrounding Putnam County, appropriate sources because Harris gathered material for his Uncle Remus stories from hearing the ballads and folktales of rural slaves. (The rustic structure makes an interesting contrast to the author's Atlanta home—the Wren's Nest—also open to visitors and the scene of scheduled storytelling sessions.) A split-rail fence encloses the cabin and a blacksmith shop which houses a giant bellows, a forge and anvil, and horseshoes, plow blades and hinges.

Inside are carved-wood dioramas depicting scenes from the Uncle Remus tales, such as "Miss Cow Falls Victim to Brer Rabbit," "Brer Fox Re-roofs His House," "Why Buzzard Is Bald," and of course, "The Tar Baby Story."

There are also paintings of Turnwold, the plantation of lawyer Joseph Addison Turner who gave Harris his first job—helping to print *The Countryman*, a weekly journal of news, poetry and essays on agriculture, politics, philosophy and humor. Harris

Woodcarvings, Uncle Remus Museum

eventually contributed to the publication. Turner's son was the model for the little boy to whom Uncle Remus tells the tales. Copies of the publication rest in one case and you can even view the ad Harris answered to land the job that would launch his career: "An active, intelligent white boy, 14 to 15 years of age, is wanted at this office to learn the printing business. March 4, 1862."

The Turnwold paintings show a large white-clapboard house with narrow pillars and surrounding picket fence and outbuildings, plus scenes of slaves picking cotton. The carvings and paintings were done by two Columbus, Georgia artists.

Artifacts portray Putnam County of the mid-1800s, most donated or loaned by local residents. Cooking gear sits by the huge fireplace and corncob pipes rest on the mantel. Irons, plates, pistols, gourds, harnesses, and axes provide details, as do a cream cooler, tooth puller, nutmeg grater, cotton plant, and Confederate money.

Harris was born in Eatonton in 1848. He grew up in poverty but learned a love of reading from his mother, and he developed a keen ear for dialect and an affection for animals. He began penning the stories for his *Atlanta Constitution* column in 1877.

Soon, newspapers across the country reprinted the pieces. He wrote about what he knew best, and he saw himself not a fashioner of fiction or folklore but a compiler of stories.

Clearly, the artifacts and art provide context for "Georgia's Aesop" and his works, all residing here in abundance. In one case, you see photos of the writer, newspaper clips, first editions of the collected stories and a copy of the *Uncle Remus Magazine*. Also present are several foreign editions of the Uncle Remus tales—translated into 27 different languages—which testify to their international popularity, as well as excellent artwork of the critters, especially Brer Rabbit. Two original watercolors from the film, *Song of the South,* donated by Walt Disney in 1964, pull the collection into the present and hint at transformation of the characters, and controversy over the tales which some lately view as racist and derogatory.

Another contemporary tangent is found in a clipping of *Atlanta Constitution* columnist Colin Campbell who wondered in print why Brer Rabbit—a world-famous product of Georgia and a creation of both blacks and whites—was not chosen for Atlanta's Olympics mascot instead of the indeterminate Whatizzit (or "Izzy").

Harris and Brer Rabbit remain winners in Eatonton where businesses bear such names as Briarpatch Office Supplies and Uncle Remus' Attic. And a more modern Turnwold, privately owned, still stands a few miles east of town.

Eatonton is an hour and 20 minutes from Atlanta via I-20 east and U.S. 441 south (exit 51 off the interstate). Turn left on Business 441 at Eatonton and go into town. The courthouse is on the right as is the Uncle Remus Museum farther down. Admission is 50 cents, 25 cents for children under 12. It's open Monday through Saturday rom 10 a.m. to noon and 1 p.m. to 5 p.m., Sundays 2 p.m. to 5 p.m.; closed Tuesdays in fall and winter. Telephone: 706/485-6856.

6. The Museum of Aviation

Flying High

THE wild blue yonder becomes more accessible in Warner Robins, Georgia, home of the **Museum of Aviation** and **Georgia Aviation Hall of Fame**.

Situated at the edge of Warner Robins Air Force Base, the facility immerses you in aviation history, especially World War II when air power came of age. Models, armament, photos, videos, interactive displays and actual aircraft put you in the thick of the action. Anyone who lived through that war or who grew up in the 1950s and early 1960s on a diet of old newsreels, Walter Cronkite narrations, *Victory at Sea* and *12 O'Clock High* may wax a bit nostalgic; anyone too young for that may skip the memories and go straight to chapter one and the amazing hardware. Local angles make the story all the more intriguing.

Several historic airplanes greet you on on arrival, including the "Georgia Peach," a C-4 cargo craft that dropped paratroops in Europe and flew "the Hump" in World War II; a B-25 Mitchell of *30 Seconds Over Tokyo* fame; a "Jolly Green Giant" Sikorsky helicopter used heavily in Vietnam; and a B-52 bomber, the Cold War backbone of the Strategic Air Command. Around the back stand a U-2 spy plane, F-4 Phantom, F-86 Sabre, and other storied aircraft.

The Phase II Building houses an almost dizzying array of exhibits. On one wall hangs a poster of "nose art"—those expressive illustrations ranging from the sexy to the sanguinary that adorned the front sections of fuselages on World War II planes. Elsewhere you'll notice a tribute to Rosie the Riveter, symbol of the female workforce that built the warplanes. At center stage is an F-15 Eagle which saw action in the Persian Gulf War, while overhead hang a Yankee Doodle glider and a PT-17 Kaydet biplane.

Exhibits of the air war in World War II feature such items as WASP flying uniforms, POW diaries, Japanese electronic gear and an actual P-47 Thunderbolt. One of the more distinctive segments recounts flying "the Hump" to supply Chinese and American fighters and discusses the relatively obscure China-Burma-India theater. You see a Japanese soldier's weapons and 1,000-knot belt (a good-luck charm), American search-and-rescue gear, an Allied flyer's survival kit, and the crossbows, machetes and other weapons used by rural Burmese. Maps, photos and a video put it all in context.

Another exhibit replicates an English airfield and yet another relates five decades of the Warner Robins airbase and its vital role in logistics and maintenance. A P-22 Recruit and a cockpit simulator help illustrate the training aspect. In addition, the Vista-Scope Theater, a large-screen cinema with wraparound sound, shows two 30-minute aviation films each hour.

The flight continues on the second floor where you see more on Warner Robins, plus aircraft art and a replica of an 1896 Chanute glider. Technology moves forward a bit at the section on electronic warfare, although an information panel notes that the first use of electronic jamming of radio transmissions dates back to the 1904 Russo-Japanese War. Here you not only learn about modern techniques to evade enemy radar and fire, but you can sit in a B-52 electronic warfare simulator and get a feel for it, too.

Also on this floor is the **Georgia Aviation Hall of Fame** honoring Georgians who played major roles in civilian and military aviation. They range from General Robert L. Scott, leader of the famed Flying Tigers, to Jackie Cochran who headed the Women's Air Force Service Pilots, and Eugene Jacques Ballard, a World War I flyer and the first black military pilot. Their achievements are reflected in plaques, photos, models and memorabilia. The hall also relates the origins of Atlanta-based Delta Airlines in the 1920s.

Hangar I contains displays on Desert Storm and forward air control operations of Vietnam vintage. It also exhibits, in gallery style, various types of aircraft engines. On view

THE MUSEUM OF AVIATION

as well are numerous helicopters, such as the Huskie and Iroquois.

Beyond in the Camouflage Building you'll find an exhibit on General Scott, an F-105 cockpit simulator (in which you're encouraged to sit) and a spy plane display. The amphitheater outside in the rear is used for concerts.

The Museum of Aviation is an hour and 45 minutes southeast of Atlanta via I-75. Depart the interstate at exit 45 onto Watson Boulevard and turn south on Route 247. The site is at the southern end of the airbase. Admission is free, but donations are welcome; there's a small fee for the VistaScope Theater. The museum is open daily 10 a.m. to 5 p.m., and picnic tables are available near the entrance.

7. Ocmulgee National Monument

Pieces of the Past, II

THE prehistoric Mississippian culture arose in the middle Mississippi Valley around A.D. 750 and spread throughout the central and eastern part of what is now the United States. The dispersion of this Native American culture, one of the most complex north of Mexico, resulted in major centers in Cahokia (Illinois) and Moundville (Alabama). Smaller communities developed in this area—along the Etowah River in northwest Georgia and on the banks of the Ocmulgee River in middle Georgia where the city of Macon now stands.

Now a national monument, the Ocmulgee site demonstrates several successive periods of Native American occupation of the area—the mound-building Mississippians, the Lamar culture encountered by Spanish explorer Hernando DeSoto in 1540, and the Creeks who settled here in the late 1600s around an early British trading post. By the mid-18th century little remained of the mound builders.

Not so today. An archeological museum and several sites on the surrounding acres tell the story of these ancient people, their agriculture-based society, and the impact of Europeans on the region. Objects excavated on the Macon Plateau include pottery, effigy pipes and gourd bowls. You'll also see copper-wrapped panther jaws, copper sun disks, beads, bone hooks, a bow and arrows, and stone and bone tools for skinning game.

These were very capable farmers, cultivating tobacco, corn, beans and squash, and on exhibit are digging sticks, stone hoes and other implements as well as clay pots for cooking and storing food. Accompanying videos illustrate pottery-making and flint-knapping.

The Mississippians dwelt in thatched houses and erected burial mounds where leaders were interred with jewelry, tools and weapons. They placed images of themselves in stone and wood statues, effigy pipes, figurines, vessels, clay cups and copper plaques, demonstrating an artistic and spiritual side as well as a practical and commercial one. Photos and dioramas provide added detail of the archeological data gleaned.

A walk through the monument's park-like environs enables you to revisit that period, after a fashion. Not far from the museum is a restored ceremonial earth lodge where religious and political leaders met. It measures 42 feet in diameter with a fire pit in the center and seating for nearly 50. A short stroll takes you to a funeral mound where excavation uncovered more than 100 burials. There's also a trading post site where in later centuries English traders swapped firearms, cloth and trinkets for furs and hides.

A longer hike goes out to the **Great Temple Mound** which stands about 45 feet high. In its day, it was topped with a rectangular wooden structure. The **Opelofa Nature Trail** winds through the bottomland along Walnut Creek. If hiking is not to your liking, you can drive your car to the more distant mounds.

Ocmulgee National Monument is located off Emery Highway, across the river from downtown Macon. It's about an hour and one-half southeast of Atlanta via I-75 and I-16. Take U.S. 80 east off I-16 and turn right on Emery Highway. Admission is free. The site is open daily 9 a.m. to 5 p.m. except Christmas and New Year's Day. There are picnic tables near the visitor center/museum. Telephone: 912/752-8257.

8. Milledgeville

A Capital Idea

ATLANTA is the latest in a line of Georgia capitals, and to step outside the Big A is to walk back in time. In the early 1800s, the capital moved from Augusta to Milledgeville, a place situated between Macon and Augusta and at the time considered the center of the state. The new capital was carved from nothing, for no settlement existed prior to this sociopolitical annointment.

First came the State Capitol building which today is part of **Georgia Military College**. In the early 1830s, some $15,000 was appropriated for a Governor's Mansion, which was built in 1835-38. It ended up costing $50,000—considerable cash in those days—but today it's worth it just to get a glimpse of the past.

The capital stood at Milledgeville from 1803 to 1868; the last governor to occupy the executive mansion was Union General Thomas Ruger. After the War Between the States and transfer of the capital to Atlanta, Milledgeville slipped into depression. The former abode of governors became a cheap hotel, and later a college dormitory. Acquired by Georgia Military College in 1879, the building was transferred in 1889 to Georgia Normal and Industrial College for Women, now **Georgia College**, and has continued as part of that school to the present. Repairs on the 15,000-square-foot edifice began in the mid-1960s.

Today a tour of the place turns up hidden stairways and compartments, exquisite furnishings, a "TV star" ballroom, and more. It's a grand walk-through of both manor and history.

You start with some historical perspective and an overview of the structure, learning that ten governors lived here and each probably modified it to suit him and his family. The best descriptions of interiors have come from letters of governor' wives. The Palladian-inspired building, designed by Charles

McClusky and built by Timothy Porter, has 32-inch-thick brick walls that were overlaid with stucco which was scored to look like massive blocks.

In a room abutting the ground-floor reception room you'll see a "secret" narrow stairway behind a closet-type door that mounts directly to the third floor. Nearby is the kitchen, with its original hearth surrounded by period implements, including a very weighty cast-iron pressure cooker and a bed warmer indented to hold a cup, for a toddy perhaps. Much of the kitchen has been modernized to serve contemporary receptions, meetings and other occasions.

The beautifully furnished living room holds a hunt board that served breakfast and, later, drinks for the hunting set. Wing chairs and a painted chest of drawers also occupy the room. Your guide explains the legend of a secret tunnel that allegedly connected the mansion with the State Capitol.

A well-worn stairway leads to the second floor where in the dining room you see a striking mirror with hand-carved gilt frame, an 1820 sideboard and a *tromp d'oeil* molding that gives the ceiling the appearance of being higher than its 14 feet. In the octagonal library/office rests a massive double-sided Chippendale desk that once belonged to the Bishop of Wales.

The elegant drawing room, where men retired to smoke cigars, drink brandy and talk politics, hosted the ball and wedding scenes in the made-for-TV movie, *The Last Surviving Confederate Widow Tells All*. Its 17th- and 18th-century antiques and twin Italian black marble fireplaces give the room a luxuriant feel.

Next comes the rotunda room with its needlepoint carpet, circular mahogany table and luminous ceiling. Four petticoat mirrors let 19th-century ladies check their hemlines. The nearby parlor was where these women repaired after dinner to converse, sing and sometimes faint. Here you'll see more needlepoint carpeting, plus a clock with a miniature harpist that actually plays and a 1700s Federal mahogany secretary with several hidden compartments for storing valuables.

Across Clarke Street from the executive mansion in a row of

college-owned Victorian buildings resides a small museum that traces the state's development in a different fashion. **The Museum and Archives of Georgia Education** is worth a peek, especially if you've got a few minutes while waiting for the governor's mansion tours which run on the half hour.

At left off the entranceway is a room filled with diverse old wooden desks—some with inkwells, all with grooves for pencils or pens. On the teacher's desk stand a handled wooden holder for 154 pencils, a stereoscope and, of course, a bell. Bookshelves hold student' texts and professional volumes for teachers, ranging from *The Pilgrim's Progress* and *Harvey's English Grammar* to *How to Teach Reading*, *Derry's History of the United States* and *How Children Learn*.

Another permanent display is the **Carl Vinson Memorial Exhibit**. Vinson represented this area in Congress for more than five decades and served for 30 years as head of the House Armed Services Committee. There are photos of the powerful congressman with LBJ, FDR, JFK, and a young Senator Sam Nunn, as well as a letter from President Harry Truman thanking Vinson for his support in dealing with General Douglas MacArthur. Mementos include glasses, gavel, straw hat, and a bayonet letter opener.

A third room and the hallway host rotating exhibits, such as Barry Moser's original wood engravings for classic children's literature and memorabilia from the Georgia State College for Women, circa 1940s.

Milledgeville is about one hour and 45 minutes from Atlanta. Take I-20 east to U.S. 441 (exit 51) south; go through Eatonton. At Milledgeville head straight on Business 441 (Columbia Street), turn left on Montgomery and right on Clarke. The Old Governor's Mansion is open Tuesday through Saturday 10 a.m. to 4 p.m., Sundays 2 p.m. to 4 p.m., closed Mondays. Admission is $3. Telephone: 912/453-4545. The Education Museum is open Monday through Friday noon to 5 p.m., Saturdays 1 p.m. to 5 p.m., and Sundays 2 p.m. to 5 p.m. Free admission. Telephone: 912/453-4391.

9. Panola Mountain

Back to Nature Nearby

THE city's where the action is, no doubt about that—the engines of commerce, culture and government running full bore. But many of us feel an occasional pull to escape the glass and concrete and call on Mother Nature. For Atlantans, that's as close as Panola Mountain State Conservation Park, less than 30 miles east of town.

Nearly one-sixth of the 167-acre site is, in fact, a mountain—a huge granite monadnock somewhat similar to **Stone Mountain**, its bulky neighbor to the north. But this is a path less traveled, less touristy, less entertainmentville. This is more refuge and oasis, with wildlife, quiet hiking trails, a multi-faceted interpretive center, and a spacious grassy apron for play and picnics.

On weekends in spring and summer Panola presents all manner of encounters of the natural kind. There are programs on bees, bats and birds of prey. Astronomy and wildflowers appear as well. Wildlife rehabilitation specialists bring in bear cubs, pos-

Araneus Diadematus

sums and other critters for lectures on preservation. One of the most popular programs is a slithery show on snakes where you see the much-maligned reptiles up close and personal—king snakes (which hunt other snakes, including the poisonous variety), hog-nose snakes, corn snakes, copperheads and rattlers, among others. Park rangers field questions about their serpentine friends and even let you caress the harmless types.

The park has three easy-going self-guided trails, ranging in length from three-quarters of a mile to one-and-three-quarters. Pathways wind through a forest of pine and mixed hardwoods and around weathered lumps of lichen-covered rock, part of the massive outcrop exposed some 15 million years ago and now home to an array of animals and rare plants. Wooden benches offer places to rest and ruminate.

On Saturdays, Sundays and major holidays the park conducts a ranger-guided hike to the top of Panola Mountain and back, a three-and-a-half mile jaunt that takes about three hours. From Memorial Day through Labor Day this gig starts at 10 a.m., in other months at 2:30 p.m. You're advised to wear comfortable shoes and clothing and, in warmer months, be wary of ticks.

The interpretive center is home to live bats, snakes and turtles, plus a hard-working beehive. It's also taxidermy heaven. An encased woodland scene contains bobcat, deer, red and gray fox, beaver, crow, racoon, mink, muskrat and more. There are also numerous stuffed raptors and a large butterfly collection.

Here, too, kids can play Panola Jackpot, an interactive touch-screen game that quizzes them about conservation. They earn points for correct answers; however, they ante up nothing but their knowledge of nature. There's also a small box where you can see the most dangerous creature in the forest.

Nearby stands a fascinating diorama explaining granite outcrops. Panola Mountain was designated a National Natural Landmark to protect the locale in response to the fact that quarrying, development and dumping have ruined so many other Georgia outcrops. A passage notes: "Only a few undamaged outcrops with some of Georgia's rarest plants exist. The fate of these rare plants is tied to the fate of the outcrops." The exhibit goes on to describe how Cladonia and Parmelia lichens and black rock moss "pioneer" plant settlements on granite shoulders. Sandwort, pineweed and Confederate daisies follow sunnybells and broomsedge. Last in the evolution come yellow jasmine and loblolly pine.

An extensive field rolls away from the interpretive center toward the parking lots. It holds picnic tables, a playground and ample space to toss a Frisbee or simply bask in the sun. The quiet here is broken only by the laughter of children and the drone of jetliners out of Hartsfield International, reaching for some altitude in the gentle Georgia sky.

All in all, the place is a near-perfect combination of park and conservation center just outside the perimeter highway. As a quick getaway from urban burdens, it's a natural.

Panola Mountain State Conservation Park lies about 40 minutes east of Atlanta. Take I-20 to exit 36. Go right on Panola Mountain Road and left on Snapfinger Road (Route 155). It's open year round and every day except Monday (unless that day is a major holiday). There's a $2 parking fee which is not charged on Wednesdays. Telephone: 770/389-7801.

Southeast Quadrant

Here and There

SOUTHEAST of Atlanta you roll through county seats which all seem to have imposing courthouses, no matter how meager the locale. The fields and farms display their rural sculpture—weathered barns with metal roofs, sagging sheds, hay rolled up like some sort of canape, livestock motionless in the fields.

The communities of Covington and Juliette have seen the light, of movie cameras, that is. Covington, off I-20, is the town-square setting for the TV series, *In the Heat of the Night*. Juliette, east of I-75 and near Jarrell Plantation, was the filming locale for *Fried Green Tomatoes* (and they are served at the Whistle Stop Cafe).

Also in the entertainment category, there's makin' music in **Macon**, home to the Allman Brothers, Otis Redding, Little Richard and others. The city plans to establish a **Georgia Music Hall of Fame** near the Macon Terminal and renovate the old **Douglass Theater** which decades back showcased black performers.

And if you're in summertime Macon and want to catch some basic baseball, check out the minor league **Macon Braves**.

Should you wander south, there are numerous antique shops in and around **Perry**. West a bit lies **Fort Valley**, literally a peach of a place; look for signs advertising peach ice cream and peach popsicles. Just off Route 49, you'll find **Massee Lane Gardens**, nine acres of camellias that bloom November through March, plus roses, azaleas, dogwoods and other springtime plants.

The **Fox Winery** in Social Circle offers tours and tastings, and you can buy monastery-made comestibles and bonsai plants at the **Monastery of the Holy Spirit** in Conyers just south of I-20.

Farther east, near Eatonton, visit **Rock Eagle**, site of a 5,000-year-old effigy made of milky quartz that measures 132 feet from wingtip to wingtip.

You can shoot the rapids and shoot the breeze elsewhere; if you're in Griffin try shooting for real. **The Cherokee Rose Shooting Resort** lets you try your hand and aim at championship sporting clays. Shotgun rentals are available.

Also in Griffin and for the agriculture-minded, the **Agricultural Experiment Station**, a unit of the University of Georgia, conducts research into peanuts, soils, food safety, horticulture, and plant diseases and will give interested parties information on the broad range of research undertaken there.

You can find several seasonal fests hereabouts. For example, each September **Barnesville Buggy Days** commemorates the carriage industry that built the town, presenting crafts, parades, antique cars and several old-time horse-drawn buggies.

Southwest of Atlanta

SOUTHWEST OF ATLANTA

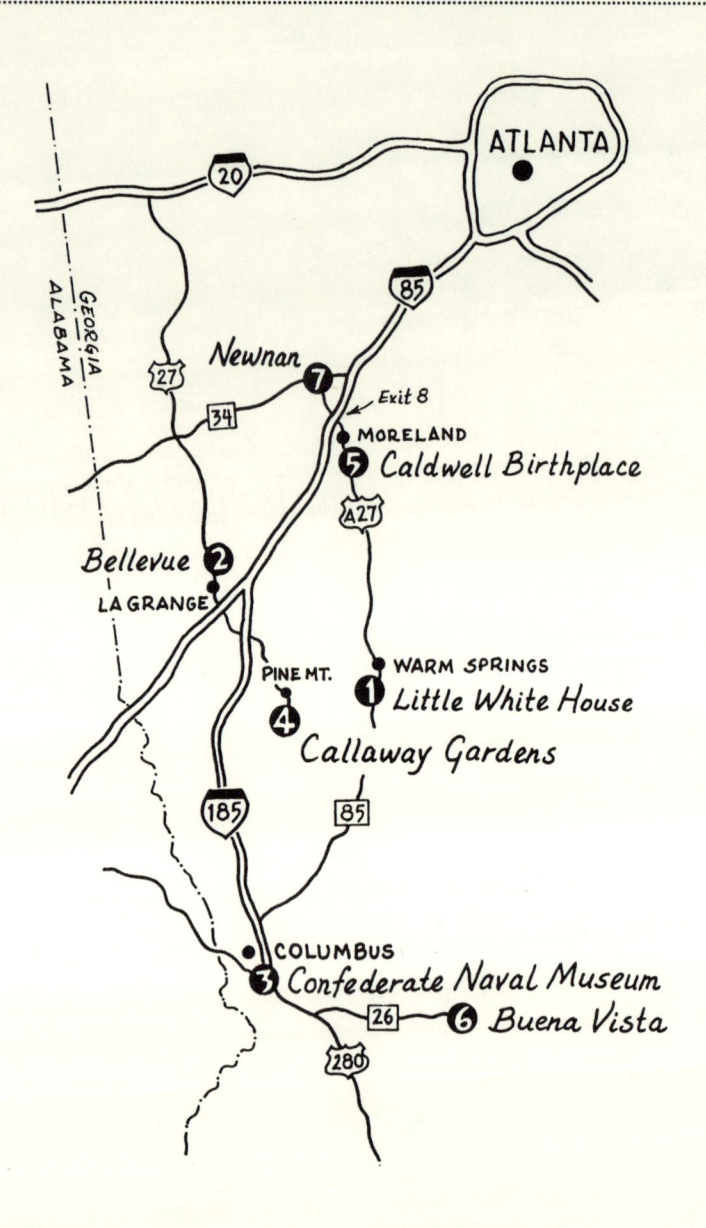

(1) The Little White House
(2) Bellevue
(3) The Confederate Naval Museum
(4) Callaway Gardens
(5) Erskine Caldwell Birthplace
(6) Buena Vista
(7) Newnan

1. The Little White House

FDR's Georgia Retreat

PROBABLY no modern President left a greater imprint than Franklin Delano Roosevelt, a man both loved and loathed during his unprecedented four terms in office. His were crisis-laden times and he hurled himself at the mighty challenges of the Depression and World War II, tirelessly toiling in national and international arenas. But probably nowhere is there a better localized portrait of a relaxed and informal FDR than at Warm Springs, Georgia.

He first visited Warm Springs in 1924 to test the therapeutic value of the local baths for his polio, and he died here on April 12, 1945, of a cerebral hemorrhage. Between those dates there were many moments of enjoyment, and you depart from his country home more uplifted than saddened. The informality, the "common touch" strike familiar chords; it becomes easier to identify with the man as opposed to the President. As much as anything, this chapter of FDR's story conveys a triumph of spirit.

The site hinges on two main exhibits, with a third in the offing. One is the Little White House itself, a clapboard cottage built in 1931-32 for about $8,000. More simple than sumptuous, cozy rather than courtly, it was the principal retreat for a President battling his own ailment and the ills of the nation. The other is a small museum created from a neighbor's home, a compact display of FDR memorabilia, especially as those items pertain to his Warm Springs sojourns. A third element is addition of a **Rural Electrification Museum** to commemorate the bringing of electricity to rural America, one of FDR's New Deal efforts and one that supposedly sprang from his residence in southwest Georgia. Plans call for a 15,000-square-foot building, with rural electrical cooperatives nationwide donating items to tell the story of the Rural Electrification Administration.

The approach to the cottage is flanked by guardhouses, one for a Marine sentry and the other designated for Secret Service. You enter through the kitchen past an old icebox. The pantry is stocked with period cooking and serving gear. At the living room/dining room you stand in the heart of the house. The bookcase here holds the very volumes it contained in April 1945. A New Deal rug covers the floor near the stone fireplace; on the mantel sits a model of a whaling ship fashioned by FDR and a bodyguard. You also see the President's unfinished portrait which was being painted at the time of his death, truly "a moment frozen in time."

Dozens of details demand inspection. The sundeck recalls the fantail of a ship (FDR had been Secretary of the Navy). The toilet in the bathroom is elevated to the height of a wheelchair. Above the front door is a ship's lantern, kept lit when he was in residence. The leash for his dog, Fala, hangs in a cabinet in the foyer.

Near the cottage are modest guest quarters for visiting VIPs.

THE LITTLE WHITE HOUSE

You also see the garage housing his 1938 blue Ford convertible, outfitted with hand controls. Beside a nearby fountain sits a 1940 Willys roadster given to him on his 58th birthday.

You reach the museum by a walkway lined with state flags, and in front of each rests a slab of native stone—petrified wood from Arizona, soapstone from Virginia, lava from Hawaii, sandstone from Illinois, granite from Vermont.

A 12-minute black-and-white film illustrates the premium FDR put on relaxation when he visited Warm Springs: picnics, horseback riding, fishing or simply conversing, be it with cabinet members, local folks or fellow polio victims. Newsreels from that era typically show FDR in motorcades or signing bills or meeting with world leaders. Here, he's taking therapy, playing modified water polo, hosting a Thanksgiving meal. One clip reveals a picnicking President with his braces on over his pants, something the public never saw.

The exhibit rooms contain gifts—such as dozens of hand-crafted canes from around the country—and personal items including a pewter cocktail shaker, ivory cigarette holder and

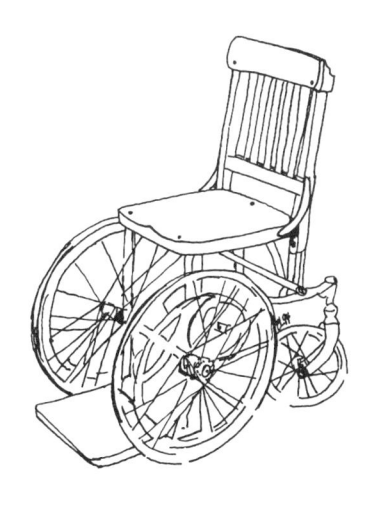

SOUTHWEST OF ATLANTA

barbering gear. A display on FDR and polio shows swimsuit, braces and a wheelchair. Another case holds a saddle and bridle.

One room presents family photos, complete with a honeymoon shot of FDR and Eleanor with this caption: "The alliance of Hyde Park and Oyster Bay portended a rich and sometimes stormy political partnership. Together they reshaped the way American government worked."

In yet a third room is the daily menu from April 12, 1945, and a poignant photographic reaction to the President's sudden death.

The whole vicinity is a memorial of sorts. Nearby **Franklin D. Roosevelt State Park** offers camping, swimming and hiking trails through the scenic forest FDR delighted in.

The most direct route to the Little White House from Atlanta is I-85 south, taking exit 8 onto Alternate U.S. 27 south. Follow that into Warm Springs and take Route 85 to the site. Travel time is about one hour and 45 minutes. It's open daily year-round from 9 a.m. to 5 p.m. Admission is $4. Telephone: 706/655-5870.

2. Bellevue

A Manor to Which You're Accustomed

THEY'RE not always easy to find in Georgia, those authentic antebellum homes boasting white columns and bespeaking white power. War, fire, decay and neglect took many of them. The city of LaGrange, however, not only claims such a mansion, but better still it belonged to a local luminary who was both a Confederate and U.S. Senator. Best of all, it's open to the public.

Bellevue, built by Benjamin Harvey Hill in the early 1850s, exquisitely represents that imposing Greek Revival architecture one equates with the Old South. It stands on a rise at the edge of the historic district and not far from downtown, its Ionic columns, spacious porticos, intricate balustrades, and elegant interior recounting a brief yet richly textured story.

Benjamin Hill was born in 1823 in Jasper County, his family farmers of modest means. He attended the University of Georgia where he was class valedictorian. He became a lawyer and did quite well in his practice, eventually purchasing 1,200 acres in LaGrange and constructing his mansion. Now it's surrounded by small, one-story houses, but 150 years ago that neighborhood consisted of Bellevue's gardens, forests and fields.

Entering state politics, Hill served in both houses of the Georgia General Assembly and went to Richmond as a senator in the Confederate government. He hastened back to Georgia in spring 1865 accompanied by Navy Secretary Stephen Mallory. Both were arrested at Bellevue by Federal troops four weeks after Appomattox.

Hill opposed post-war Union policy and military rule, but he subsequently recommended acceptance of Reconstruction; otherwise, he felt, Federal occupation would last forever. For that stance he was labeled a traitor and vilified to the extent that in

1869 he moved to Athens. He later served in the U.S. House and Senate from Georgia, a "silver-tongued orator" who died in 1882 from cancer of the tongue. He has been called a proponent of the "New South," and it's said he influenced the Hays Administration to remove Federal troops from the region.

Today Bellevue says as much about the era and the place as it does about the man. The McLendon family owned it during the last quarter of the 19th century and first quarter of the 20th. By 1930 it stood vacant, but it was saved by the Fuller E. Callaway Foundation and restored in 1975. Few family items invest the house; most furnishings are antiques purchased in New York, New Orleans, Natchez and elsewhere. The LaGrange Women's Club maintains and preserves the mansion. On-site caretakers give well-informed tours.

Design of Bellevue came from a catalogue, and actual construction was accomplished by slave labor, right down to the intricate woodwork. It's larger now due to kitchen and serving facilities in the rear that cater to banquets, teas, receptions, and meetings—functions for which the place can be rented.

The splendid entranceway has a customized wall covering that faithfully replicates the original. A crystal lantern has replaced the candle-lit chandelier of that period. Napoleon III furniture occupies this space, along with Iranian hand-loom carpets. You can still see the original plaster ceiling medallions, high baseboards and ornate cornices over the doorways. A portrait of Hill gazes down from one wall.

To the right is a double parlor with sliding doors that divided it into post-prandial rooms for men and women. With doors open it was transformed into a ballroom, its French doors opening onto the front porch. Black carrera marble forms the fireplace, and on the mantel stand Wedgewood candleholders.

Across the entranceway, the living and dining rooms have fireplaces of white Georgia marble. You see a square grand piano of rosewood, Benjamin's wedding gift to his wife. (The piano, so the story goes, was found under the back porch, half buried in dirt.) The walls hold steel engravings of Confederate generals, some of whom—along with President Jefferson Davis— are believed to have met here. Antiques ranging from a 1760 French chest to a 1795 English tea caddy enrich these rooms.

Brass rods hold down the runner on the stairway which mounts to the second floor where visitors can view two of the four bedrooms, one of which holds a rare half-tester bed and the other a melodeon.

The broad upper hallway is home to a couple of display cases containing old photos, period clothing, family mementos and some of Hill's correspondence. There are also books, including a biography of Hill written by his son, and a copy of the *Atlanta Constitution* of August 17, 1882 with a front-page story of the statesman's death.

To reach Bellevue, take I-85 south to U.S. 27 and follow that road into LaGrange. Take Broad Street across the top of the square and turn right on Ben Hill Street just before LaGrange College. Travel time from Atlanta is about one hour and 15 minutes. Admission is $3. Bellevue is open Tuesday through Saturday 10 a.m. to noon and 2 p.m. to 5 p.m., and by appointment. Closed Sundays, Mondays and holidays. Telephone: 706/884-1832.

3. The Confederate Naval Museum

Ironclads and Iron Will

QUICKLY now, can you name a Civil War ship other than the *Monitor* or *Merrimack*? Well, swabbies, there was much more to naval engagement during the conflict than that, and you can learn about the secessionist side at the Confederate Naval Museum in Columbus, about 120 miles from Atlanta and more than 200 miles from the sea.

Why a naval museum in Columbus? Rivers were transportation arteries and battlegrounds, too, and cities upstream often served as shipping centers. Columbus sits at the head of the navigable part of the Chattahoochee River which eventually flows into the Gulf of Mexico. A manufacturing town prior to the war, it converted most of its textile mills and iron works to war production—tents, swords, mortars, cannon, uniforms, and especially steam boilers for boats. Another and perhaps more important reason derives from the salvage of two sunken warships in the river below Columbus a century after the war.

The South had comparatively little in the way of a navy when the conflict began and its coastal cities endured blockade for most of the struggle. It relied on innovation, daring and determination. The 3,000-man navy employed mines and rifled cannon, ran blockades, raided sea lanes, and introduced submarines and armored ships. These tactics were not without effect. The Confederates reportedly sank 200 Union vessels during the war.

Outside the museum you're dramatically greeted by the salvaged wrecks of the *CSS Chattahoochee*, a 130-foot-long sail/steam-powered gunboat, and the *CSS Jackson*, a 224-foot-long ironclad ram. Anchor, fantail, propeller, and 9-inch shells accompany the skeletal remains. Standing nearby like muscular bodyguards are sleek, black Brooke rifled cannon.

The compact museum relies heavily on ship models, such as a

large-scale version of the *CSS Virginia* (*née Merrimack*), the first ironclad, which in 1862 sank the *USS Cumberland* and ushered in the age of iron warships. Its low profile and sloping sides gave it a sinister, predatory appearance. Yet another model on view is the blockade-runner *Mary Bowers*.

Display cases exhibit ordnance such as grape shot, gun-carriage lever and percussion fuses, and weapons such as cutlasses, bayonets and boarding pikes—rusted and worn but grim and deadly nonetheless. Another exhibit focuses on the Columbus operations, displaying steam gauges, brass fittings, drawings and plans from the Naval Iron Works, and a painting of its commander, Chief Engineer James H. Warner.

There are also examples of the two-inch-thick armor plate that outfitted 25 ironclads, including the *CSS Savannah* and *CSS Tennessee*. The Confederacy had another two dozen in planning or production at war's end. A diagram and a cutout model reveal these vessels' cramped quarters.

Then there's the *CSS Hunley*, the first submarine to sink an enemy ship in combat—on February 17, 1864 in Charleston Harbor. It used a torpedo hitched to an elongated nose spar. Paintings, plans and a model of the mini-sub tell its pioneering if ill-fated story. Immediately after its historic hit, the *Hunley* vanished off the South Carolina coast, with the loss of all hands.

Special attention is given to the *Jackson* and the *Chattahoochee*, among only a handful of preserved Civil War vessels. The latter was scuttled to prevent capture and the formrer was seized by Federal troops and burned in the river. Tongs, hooks, wrenches, rudder, spikes, a ventilation grate, and other recovered artifacts bear historical witness. Photos illustrate the 1964 salvage effort.

Numerous paintings and prints portray the Confederate Navy in action, including the fierce Battle of Mobile Bay and the inconclusive engagement between the *Monitor* and *Merrimack/Virginia*. Rosters, maps, flags, uniforms and news clippings all add context. And even if you can name vessels other than the *M* and *M*, you'll glean bits of fascinating trivia. For example, the Confederacy had its own naval academy in Virginia. The *USS Cairo* was the first of 40 Union vessels destroyed by mines or torpedoes; it was sunk in Mississippi's Yazoo River in 1862—and was raised virtually intact a century later to be displayed at Vicksburg National Military Park. Then there was the *CSS Georgia*, engaged in the Confederacy's only "foreign battle"—a cannon barrage against attacking tribesmen in Morocco.

An interesting adjunct to the museum is the restored **Columbus Iron Works** building on the other side of the Columbus historic district, about ten blocks north of the museum. Now a 77,000-square-foot trade and convention center, the structure retains its magnificent historic cast with old brick, massive timbers, exposed ceiling and sculpture-like gears and pulleys. Next door is **Arsenal Place** which housed the old drop forge and warehouse of the iron works.

Operated by the Georgia Historical Commission, the Confederate Naval Museum is located on U.S. 280 next to the home field of the Red Stix, a minor league baseball team. Take I-85 south to I-185 and follow it to exit 1, Victory Drive (U.S. 280) going west. Driving time from Atlanta is about one hour and 55 minutes. No admission fee, but donations are welcome. It's open year-round (except Mondays and major holidays) Tuesday through Friday 10 a.m. to 5 p.m., Saturday and Sunday 1 p.m. to 5 p.m. Telephone: 706/327-9798.

4. Callaway Gardens

Butterflies Flutter By

CALLAWAY Gardens in Pine Mountain, Georgia is a finely sculpted, multifaceted playground featuring golf, tennis, fishing, water sports, skeet shooting and summertime spectaculars. But amid the recreational bounty is a natural bonanza, two very special enclosures where the flora and fauna are fantastic and are themselves worth the drive and price of admission.

The five-acre **Sibley Horticultural Center** comprises several diverse gardens, beginning with a tropical environment. Here you're welcomed by bottlebrush, philodendron, firecracker flowers, cast iron plant, and Persian violets. Palm fronds splinter the sunlight. Temperature remains above 60 degrees Fahrenheit to make these plants feel at home.

Next comes the rock wall garden where your path winds past caladium, blue ginger, asparagus fern, brake fern, azaleas, camel-

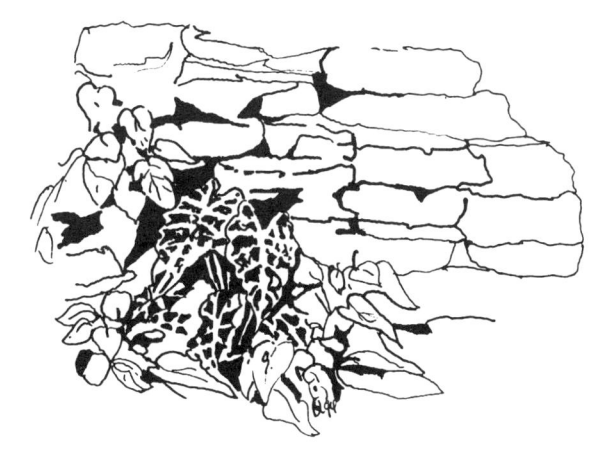

Tropical Plants, Sibley Center

lias, and banks of English ivy. Folding doors standing 24 feet high and weighing 1,600 pounds protect this and adjacent plots which are cooled by fans, windows and a misting system. Some 300 tons of Tennessee fieldstone form the garden walls. To the left and outside is the sculpture garden, a swatch of hedge-bounded lawn surrounding a smooth, milky chunk of carrera marble.

The course continues up to a 22-foot-high waterfall behind which nestles a grotto where grow pothos, hybrid orchids and the lovely tropical American tailflower, or Lady Jane.

You then descend into the floral conservatory with its stunning layout of flower beds, ivy and trees. Creeping fig covers a rock wall, eliciting an image of some forgotten Mayan temple. And there is an international cast to this area; for instance, a small hillside of Norfolk Island pine from Australia and a weeping podocarpus tree from East Africa.

The open garden beyond the doors and canopy offers a brilliant array in summer—plumed cockscomb, globe amaranth, African marigold, purple heart, iris, columbine, salvia, fountain grass, silver-dollar plant, Russian sage, lantana, cigar flower and more, all flanked by a platoon of magnolia trees.

Plenty of benches permit visitors to stop, sit and smell the roses. And it goes without question that photo ops are many.

You focus, as was intended, on the integrated indoor and outdoor settings and not on the structure and its energy conservation techniques. Nor do you see much of the many production greenhouses that enable the center to turn botanically with the seasons. But you most assuredly will appreciate the results.

Back along the shady Scenic Drive, you arrive at the **Day Butterfly Center**, a 7,500-square-foot polygonal conservatory where butterflies flutter by, over and around, sometimes alighting on your head or on a leaf in front of your face. They cling to the screen walls and tree branches, too, but on the wing they're a little like confetti kept aloft by breezes. Some 50 species of tropical butterflies inhabit this oversize collector's cup where it seems nature has put flowers to flight. Their lifespan is two to eight weeks, and there may be 1,000 at a time living within the conservatory. Some butterflies flit about in groups of three or four but most fly solo. There are a few as small as a nickel and others the size of a bird.

Informational signs along the pathways and amid the greenery provide details on these delicate creatures. For example, each type of butterfly seeks a specific host plant on which to deposit its eggs. Butterflies are most active in warm sunlight, tending to perch on cloudy days and late in the afternoon.

And the *lepidoptera* are not alone here. The conservatory also is a haven for bleeding heart doves, mandarin ducks and other tropical birds.

The center, which opened in 1988, is more than a winged symphony; it presents a short video on butterflies as well as displays on topics such as metamorphosis and camouflage. A world map points out butterfly habitats, with the Amazon basin claiming the greatest diversity—one particular square-mile area holds 1,000 species. Georgia is home to more than 160 varieties, including the buckeye, black swallowtail, cloudless sulphur and pearl crescent—and you may see some of the natives outside in the expanse of gardens. Tropical butterflies are reared at farms both here and abroad. One exhibit depicts the four stages of a butterfly's life and another tells how to start a butterfly garden.

Popular with visitors, the Day Butterfly Center also has received professional acclaim. In 1994 the Georgia Society of Professional Engineers selected it as one of the state's ten top engineering achievements of the past 50 years.

Callaway Gardens is owned and operated by the Ida Cason Callaway Foundation, dedicated to horticulture, charity, religion, education and science. It's about an hour and a half south of Atlanta. Take I-85 south to exit 5. Follow I-185 south to exit 14 and proceed south on U.S. 27 to Pine Mountain. Callaway offers nature trails, bicycle paths and 700 varieties of azaleas that blaze beautifully in spring. It's also the Southern filming location for public television's **The Victory Garden.** *General admission is $15 per car on weekdays, $20 per car on weekends, which gives entry to the gardens, the horticultural center, the butterfly center and the beach. Calloway is open seven days, 7 a.m. to 7 p.m. in summer, then closing earlier as daylight fades. Telephone: 800/282-8181.*

5. Erskine Caldwell Birthplace

Author's Little Acre

NOVELIST Erskine Caldwell portrayed his native South in hardscrabble hues and he pulled no punches in creating story lines and characters filled with lust, pride, hypocrisy, cruelty, craziness and other colorful human attributes. Landscapes were coarse, stingy and tough. His perspective did not endear him to his fellow Southerners in the 1930s and 1940s, and a half century later, when some folks in Moreland, Georgia wanted to commemorate Caldwell by restoring his birthplace, they encountered lingering disapproval and defensiveness.

But they proceeded nonetheless, and a short drive to Moreland today, about an hour south of Atlanta and just below Newnan, puts you in Caldwell's cradle—a five-room house built by local farmers for the resident Presbyterian pastor, who was Erskine's father, Ira. The structure was was moved from neighboring White Oak in 1990 and restoration started shortly thereafter.

The writer-to-be was born in this humble frame dwelling in 1903 and reared in it until age 3. The family moved to South Carolina, then back to Georgia near Augusta. As a young man Caldwell worked as a stringer for the *Augusta Chronicle*, and subsequently was a reporter for the *Atlanta Journal* at the same time that Margaret Mitchell worked for that paper. In 1927, he moved to Maine to write full time. With publication of *Tobacco Road* in 1932 and *God's Little Acre* the following year he became a best-selling author. He wrote with passion and with humor, and he was one of the first Southern writers to examine the Depression's impact on the region. As one biographer has noted, his central concern was with poverty in its "material, moral, social, and spiritual manifestations."

His writings and career, a few personal objects and testimony to his mark are the main appeal here. The house itself is unremarkable and contains only a few period pieces, rather than actual furnishings or other items from Caldwell's youth. You see the original pine woodwork, floors and ceiling, as well as the brick fireplace. A hand-fashioned wooden latch on one door underscores the rustic utility of the dwelling. It hadn't been lived in for quite some time prior to reclamation; in fact, it reportedly stored hay and farm equipment as late as 1989.

But it's not simply Caldwell's house. The grassroots effort at restoration was aimed at preserving the sense of place the writer portrayed in his books about the rural South. Still, it's more author than abode. A couple of bookshelves showcase his works—copies of his novels in French, German, Japanese, Italian and other tongues. All told, his works were translated into more than two dozen languages. He was immensely popular with foreign readers; indeed, one Japanese critic observed that American GIs in occupied Japan after World War II read his books and "planted Caldwellian seeds in the Japanese earth." His books sold more than 80 million copies worldwide, but most have been out of print for some time. A couple of regional university presses are reportedly bringing some titles back into circulation.

In addition to Caldwell's books and various mementos, you'll see his hat, jacket, Smith-Corona typewriter, briefcase with English-Spanish dictionary, and a wedding ring (he was married four times). Photos, quotes and historical data line the walls in a couple of rooms, and there are lurid posters advertising movies made from his books. One of the quotes serves as a rebuttal of sorts to offended Southerners: "I had no intention at all to try to make the South look worse than it was. But I never considered myself a spokesman for the South either. I think everybody has the right to give his own version of life, and I was just giving mine."

The museum hopes to acquire video equipment to show taped interviews with Caldwell. Also, it loans some of its panels to small-town libraries around the state so that more people can become acquainted with Caldwell and his works.

About 30 yards from "the Little Manse," as it's called, stands the **Old Mill Museum** containing pre-1940 farm and household implements, the sort of gear that worked the land and sheds and homes of the rural South that Caldwell knew. The structure was a textile mill from the late 1800s to the mid-1900s. Here you find harnesses, an anvil, swing churn, spinning wheel, old well with a milk rope, buggy foot warmer, cotton duster, restored cider mill, mule-drawn hay mower and plows, and scales for weighing cotton, among other artifacts.

Nearby is a building that's scheduled to house photos, clothing, typewriters, and other memorabilia of Moreland native son Lewis Grizzard, an *Atlanta Journal-Constitution* columnist and humorist who died in early 1994.

To reach Moreland take I-85 south to exit 8, then follow U.S. 29 into town. Turn right on East Camp Street. The Caldwell House is on the left just before the railroad tracks. Admission for adults is $2, children $1. It's open Saturdays and Sundays 1 p.m. to 4 p.m., or by appointment. Telephone: 770/251-4438.

6. Buena Vista

State of the Arts and Music

DRIVING south from Atlanta a couple of hours or so can put you in Buena Vista, pronounced *Byew*na vista (and Houston is *How*ston and Lafayette is *Luh*fayit—but hey, this is Georgia, not Mexico, Texas or France), where the arts are alive and well and...different.

The music here is country-western and the painting a bit bizarre. A shrine to the former sits on the square; a showcase of the latter resides outside of town, but seeing it is well worth the ride.

Could this small agricultural community become another Branson, Missouri (sometimes known as Nashville West)? Sing along: In 1992 apparel executive Mike Moon brought his **National Country Music Hall of Fame** down here from Pigeon Forge, Tennessee ("So long, Dolly...") while also relocating his **Elvis Presley Museum** here and launching the **Silver Moon Music Barn** and the gospel-driven **Front Porch Music Hall**.

The NCMHF has recycled an old brick cotton warehouse, a most compatible adaptation. Country music tunes play in the background as you wander through on a self- guided tour. The country-western ambience is reinforced by walls and panels hung with saddles, bridles, farm implements and dated automotive gear.

The familiar and expected are juxtaposed with the unfamiliar and unanticipated. Your journey starts near a delapitated but authentic moonshine still, rigged to run off propane as well as wood. Next to it is daredevil descendant Robbie Kneivel's record-setting jump cycle. There's a wonderful array of instruments on hand. Among them: Tom T. Hall's fiddle and bow, Merle Haggard's Stella Harmony guitar, an accordion of Pee Wee King, a Homer and Jethro mandolin, Grandpa Jones' banjo, Mother Maybelle Carter's autoharp, a Buck Owens guitar, and a

Univox electric guitar once used by both Johnny Cash and Elvis Presley in RCA recording sessions.

This is show biz after all, and you're reminded of that by the glitzy stage costumes of Margo Smith, Ronnie Milsap, Dolly Parton and Barbara Mandrell. There are star' hats, boots and jackets, even a pair of Linda Ronstadt's jogging shorts. In one display case you see a Hank Williams Jr. bowling ball and in another Tanya Tucker's 10-speed bicycle.

And just when you feel sated, you come across an autographed "first dollar" that Elvis reportedly placed in a Mississippi church collection plate during a revival meeting. (Moon paid $8,000 for that dollar in 1982.) Then there's Barbara Mandrell's silver-gray Jaguar, smashed by another vehicle in September 1984, injuring family members and almost ending her career. And speaking of transportation, you'll also gaze upon a 1967 Continental that was The King's very own, a 1969 Cadillac owned by Hank Willliams Jr. and a 1954 Caddy that belonged to Jerry Lee Lewis.

You're transported to a different realm altogether when you drive out to **Pasaquan**, former home/stage/canvas/temple of Eddie Owens Martin, *aka* St. EOM (a moniker formed by his initials and pronounced St. Ohm). He was born into a sharecropper family in 1908 and raised here in Marion County. At age 14 he ran away to New York City where he got his education on the streets of the ripening Roaring Twenties Big Apple. He was a hustler, gambler, fortune-teller and artist, among other trades. Returning to Georgia in the 1950s, he built Pasaquan—a four-acre compound of walls, pagodas, minarets, walkways and structures that might variously be described as colorful, wild, freaky, far out, eye-popping, or psychedelic. Arts writer/editor and St. EOM biographer Tom Patterson has said of it, "Pasaquan is the culmination of Eddie Owens Martin's self-reinvention" and called it "one of the great masterworks of American visionary vernacular architecture."

Martin may not have moved much art in New York, but here he could create to his eccentric heart's content, and he did. And he died here in 1986 of a self-inflicted gunshot wound. More

Pasaquan

recently the local historical society has partially restored the place. In addition to touring, it can be rented for receptions and meetings, and reportedly proved the perfect spot for a convention of Atlanta psychotherapists. The long-term plan involves completing work on the grounds and house and exhibiting some of St. EOM's art now in storage.

Pasaquan itself is a piece of work, and no brief account can do it justice. Watchful totemic faces. Walls pulsating with suns, scrolls, wheels, orbs, and geometric patterns. Colors bright, energetic and potent. Near a passage through one side wall you see a pair of erect, life- size, very male and female figures, each holding two red-painted human heads by the hair. An elevated structure near the entrance has steps leading down to a sand pit. The entire side of another structure is mostly occupied by a pair of hypnotic eyes.

St. EOM—given to wearing turbans, braids, boots, and brilliantly hued robes—supposedly was influenced by Mexican temples ruins and images of the lost Atlantis, but it's no stretch to read in some Hindu, Egyptian and Californian.

BUENA VISTA

A voice from "the spirit world" once told Eddie Owens Martin that he'd start something new, that he'd be a Pasaquoyan. He surely started something different, and seeing is believing.

You can reach Buena Vista via I-85 south to I-185 and to U.S. 280 in Columbus, then by following Route 26 east. Or take I-75 south briefly and get on Route 85 at Riverdale, then follow that south to Manchester and take Route 41 from there to Buena Vista. Travel time from Atlanta is a tad over two hours. Pasaquan lies six miles north of town; go out Route 137 to county road 78 and turn right. It's open Saturdays 10 a.m. to 6 p.m. and Sundays 1 p.m. to 6 p.m., or weekdays by appointment. Adults $5, seniors $3, under 12 free. Telephone: 912/649-9444. The National Country Music Hall of Fame, situated on the square, is $3. Hours are Monday through Saturday 10 a.m. to 6 p.m. and Sundays 1 p.m. to 6 p.m. Telephone: 912/649-2259. (NOTE: The NCMHF also gives information about performances at the Silver Moon and Front Porch Music Hall.)

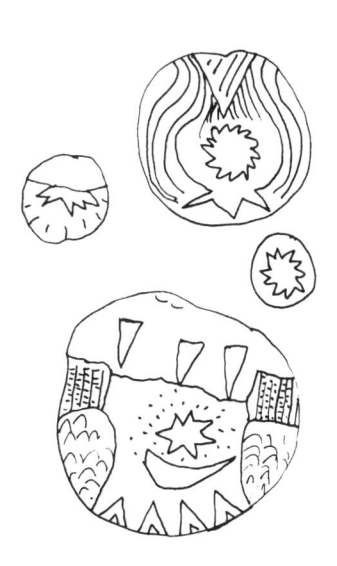

7. Newnan

An Education in Architecture

THEY call it "the city of homes," and not without reason. Newnan, Georgia, less than 45 minutes below Atlanta, boasts an outstanding assortment of Federal, Colonial, Greek Revival, Victorian, and Craftsman homes. The official driving tour counts 23 structures throughout the community. In addition, **Oak Grove** and **Catalpa** plantation homes are open for tours by appointment. On the last weekend of each April, the Newnan-Coweta County Historical Society holds a walk-through tour of selected private residences in one of the city's five historic districts and including the magnificent county courthouse.

On the annual tour is a museum that's a former home and originally a school. Located at the corner of Temple and College streets in one of the lovely old neighborhoods, the **Male Academy Museum** offers its own architectural lesson. Each year it hosts a course for local fifth graders to study Newnan's treasured architecture.

The museum itself is a study. Established in 1840 as a private boys' school for grades one through six, the place served an educational role untl 1883. Subsequently it was converted to a duplex and became a private residence for nearly a century. In 1974 restoration transformed it back to its initial appearance, complete with cupola. Inside, exhibits let you peer into Newnan's past.

A small room on the left reflects the building's first use. Rows of archaic desks and benches rest on the old heart pine floor. Period texts and literature fill the bookcases. Along the back wall you see photos of Georgia schools from the late 1800s and early 1900s. Articles and artifacts include a teacher's bell and a prototypical lunch box—a small, covered tin pail that might have held a potato or chunk of bread.

Across the hall is the Ira Ellis Smith collection, items from a pioneer family who moved to Newnan from Virginia by wagon in 1821. There's a lovely sideboard, plus a rope bed with hand-carved headboard posts, a fine corner cabinet, a pewter condiments holder, a hand-dyed rug, and family photos.

In the larger room you'll find rotating exhibits from the museum's collections; for example, a textiles display featuring 19th- and early 20th-century clothing, including antique wedding dresses. Another comprises Civil War era weapons consisting of pikes, sabers, cutlasses, rifles, cannon shot, flintlock boot pistol, Bowie knife, and bayonets (including the "dead man's hook"—a bayonet with bent blade to drag bodies from the battlefield).

The "city of homes" was the city of hospitals during the war, with some half-dozen buildings converted to facilities for treating Union and Confederate casualites. One exhibit shows a period cot as well as rubber tourniquet, amputation knife, saw, brush, scalpels, even a leg bone.

They take their history seriously here, but one establishment employs more than a touch of humor. **General Wheeler's Mess Tent and War of Northern Aggression Bookstore**, just off the square, offers food for thought and stomach. The bookshop, actually a small room, sells maps, posters, books and pamphlets related to the war. Proprietor Russ Styanoff named the deli after General Joseph Wheeler who successfully defended the city against Union troops, thereby preserving some of its architectural heritage. A 24-pound mortar greets you inside the door and Confederate weaponry and regalia adorn the walls. Sandwiches are named for prominent figures—the Nathan Bedford Forrest is a pastrami and Swiss concoction captioned on the menu, "This is the only way a Yankee could get his hands on that 'Devil' Forrest." There's molasses pie for dessert and the root beer is homemade. A sign in the window notes, "Paroled Yankees Permitted."

Newnan is about 40 miles southwest of Atlanta via I-85 and Route 34 (take exit 9 off the interstate). Go left on Jackson Street and right on Temple to reach the Male Academy Museum, admission $2, under 12 free. It's open Tuesday through Thursday 10 a.m. to 3 p.m., Saturday and Sunday 2 p.m. to 5 p.m.; closed Monday and Friday. (NOTE: The April homes tour fee is $10 in advance, $12 on the day; allow a whole afternoon.)

Southwest Quadrant

Here and There

KUDZU-COVERED trees, their hunched, rounded, vaguely ominous shapes—topiary from the Twilight Zone—seem to watch your passage along these highways and byways as well as others outside the city. It's not true that kudzu vines can cover you while you nap of an afternoon, but if you leave your car near a patch overnight, well....

In this quadrant watch for a couple of major festivals. Each spring the **Renaissance Faire** off I-85 near Fairburn reprises the age of Henry VIII (or thereabouts) with swordsmanship, pageantry, contests, games, skits, jugglers and jesters, crafts and drumsticks and flagons of ale. Some reasonably authentic jousting takes place as well. And each Labor Day weekend in Newnan the **Powers Crossroads Fair** erupts entertainingly with cloggers, bluegrass music, gospel singing, arts and crafts, and down-home country cooking. A grist mill and blacksmith shop are among the old-time trades exhibits.

If you'd like to see the "boys of summer" in their apprenticeship form, consider the **Red Stix**, the minor league baseball team in Columbus. And if you're in that city and feeling gung-ho, march over to the **National Infantry Museum** at Fort Benning.

Should a more peaceable, creative frame of mind hold sway, LaGrange invites you to check out the **Chattahoochee Valley Art Museum** and the **Lamar Dodd Art Center**.

Closer to Atlanta, **Sweetwater Creek State Park** offers five miles of pleasant hiking trails along the rippling stream where you'll also see ruins of a Civil War era textile mill. Uncovered in this wooded countryside in 1909 was a mysterious 600-pound monolith carved with a figure right out of *Chariots of the Gods*, a find that still lacks a conclusive definition.

Back in the City

A Few Suggestions

THE purpose of this book has been to introduce you to the realms beyond; to inform you about the many things to see and do outside Atlanta's perimeter. But what about the city itself? You can find all manner of official, semi-official and unofficial guides to Atlanta proper, and the intent is not to duplicate them here. But here's a taste of some key attractions (and a few that are not so well known).

Topping the list are the **Martin Luther King, Jr. Center for Nonviolent Social Change**, featuring photos and videos of Dr. King's life and times; the **CNN Center**, where news of the world goes out to the world (and studio tour lines can be long); and the city's science museum known as **SciTrek**, where the exhibits are hands-on and personal. Others include the **High Museum of Art**, a work of art in itself at 1280 Peachtree Street, and the creative and fun **ZooAtlanta** in Grant Park.

What follows are some less-heralded places, a few local "musts" and some personal favorites. And keeping in mind the spirit of this book, here's an example of an in-town day trip that demonstrates what you can do if you improvise and map out your own itinerary:

Start at Auburn Avenue, just south and east of the heart of town. "Sweet Auburn," once black Atlanta's commercial and entertainment hub, is where you now can visit the King Center, **Dr. King's Birthplace, Ebenezer Baptist Church** and the **APEX Museum** (APEX means Afro-American Panoramic Experience). Everything's within a couple of blocks of the corner of Auburn and Jackson Street. Then move a bit north and east to North Highland Avenue and the **Carter Presidential Center**, an architecturally serene yet active institution that includes a museum introducing you to the peanut farmer turned President. It highlights his political career and achievements and his much-admired ongoing work for world peace.

The Carter Center is located but a few blocks from Atlanta's first suburb, **Inman Park**, today a yuppie enclave of restored Victorian homes. And at its fringe near the MARTA station you'll find **Burton's Grill**, a legendary no-frills place serving quintessential fried chicken and other Southern favorites.

In turn, it's a hop, skip and barely a jump to **Little Five Points** (at Moreland and Euclid avenues), which takes you right back to the hippie Sixties with its cluster of funky shops and funky folks. It's Atlanta's own Haight or Soho. Again, a few blocks north resides another distinctive neighborhood, one more mainstream but loose and easy nonetheless. **Virginia-Highland** has a high concentration of informal eateries, cafes and pubs (good bets are **Murphy's** and **R.J.'s Wine Bar**) as well as artsy shops and a well-used beach volleyball court. You'll soon discover that Atlanta is more than glass and steel and commerce, and this entertaining junket is all in a day's trip.

One of the city's newer attractions is the **Atlanta History Museum** in Buckhead, north of downtown. Part of the Atlanta History Center, it offers several rotating exhibits—for example, Civil War soldiering, multi-ethnic Atlanta, myths of *Gone with the Wind*—and a fascinating journey through the city's evolution called "Metropolitan Frontier" which takes you from 1830s railroad terminus to today's Olympic host city.

The **Buckhead** commercial district is wall-to-wall cafes, clubs, restaurants, bistros, bars and boutiques. You can find French, Italian, Indian, Southwestern, as well as **Oxford Books**, possibly the best-stocked bookstore in the Southeast. An Anglo-Gaelic sidelight here might involve a pub crawl from the **Rose & Crown** to **Churchill's** to **McDuff's**, a handful of watering holes where some customers take their pints and darts seriously. If you take late-night dessert seriously, you can't beat the souffles at **Hedgerose Heights**, a top-rated restaurant where you don't need reservations to sample the chef's confection du jour.

Microbreweries and brew pubs have been a long time coming to Atlanta, due in part to quirky state laws, but the former

BACK IN THE CITY

arrived in mid-1994 with the tapping of **Marthasville Brewery** and **Atlanta Brewing Company**. Several brew pubs have now cropped up, in time to slake Olympic thirsts.

If blues and jazz are appealing rhythms, you'll find the joints jumpin' in **Kenney's Alley**, adjacent to the lively downtown shopping district called **Underground Atlanta**. To discover real Old South country fare, try **Mary Mac's** at 224 Ponce de Leon in midtown, where you can sample side dishes ranging from hoppinjohn to steamed okra and turnip green pot likker.

You can see the city, or parts of it, from auto, MARTA rapid transit, shanks mare, even horse-drawn carriage. The more athletic might rent rollerskates and single-speed bicycles at Skate Escape near **Piedmont Park**, putting wheels if not wings on your feet. But speaking of wings, a different way to see the city is from bird's-eye level: at Peachtree-DeKalb Airport, you can hire a Cessna four-seater (Historic Air Tours) or a Bell chopper (UK/USA) for flights over the metro heartbeat.

Back to some personal favorite things to do. Dramatically speaking, try **Theater Gael** or the **Horizon Theater** for uncommon performances at affordable prices. **Chastain Park** in summer is unbeatable for concerts under the stars, both soft rock and Atlanta Symphony style. Bring your own candles and picnic supper.

The Center for Puppetry Arts at 1404 Spring Street not only presents performances but also has a museum housing one of the largest collections of puppets in North America— more than 150 hand, string, rod, shadow and body puppets from around the world—and includes a hands-on, interactive gallery for kids.

The **Herndon Home** near the campus of Morris Brown College was designed and built in 1905-1910 by Alonzo F. Herndon, Atlanta barber, businessman and former slave who became one of the wealthiest blacks in the nation. Educator/activist W.E.B. DuBois called the 13-room columned mansion "the pride of black Atlanta."

The Institute of Paper Science and Technology at the edge of the Georgia Tech campus houses a fine little collection in its **Dard Hunter Paper Museum**, illustrating pre-automated paper manufacture from cultures and countries worldwide, plus early European currencies, Korean colored paper, early textbooks, scale models of pulp mills, a paper press and more.

Art and history merge at the **Cyclorama** in Grant Park. This huge, precise painting-in-the-round (50 feet high and 400 feet in circumference) depicting the 1864 Battle of Atlanta was made in 1885-1886. Wonderfully restored, it represents one of a handful of cyclorama canvases surviving from the late 19th century when they served as a popular, prototypical documentaries.

If pounding the concrete makes you yearn for a softer path and greener environs, escape from downtown and take an easy stroll along Atlanta's waterway at the **Chattahoochee River National Recreation Area.** You can choose from nine trails ranging from three to six miles, but one path less traveled by is the Powers Island route—close to the river but not too lengthy and with a whimsical touch of the unexpected. The so-called **River Dumpsite Gallery** atop a steep embankment just above an old pump house is a jungle-like grove where some enterprising, creative individual has fashioned sculpture from local junk—springs, bolts, chair frames, car bumpers, air filters, bottles, duct pipe, and Lord knows what else. A bit of Finster inspiration? Who knows? The sign only says, "Free to Browse—No Donations Please."

Folks often want to know where the peach trees are on Peachtree Street. Truth is, there are be more streets and buildings in Atlanta with Peachtree in their names than the trees themselves.

The best way to see any city is up close and personal, on foot and open-minded, bias off and hands on. Atlanta is New South, Old South, other South, and sometimes not South at all.

Finally, if your sense of wander or a fascination with things Southern lures you even farther afield, you might pick up *Discovering Dixie* by Richard Polese. It takes you on a three-week guided adventure through eight states of the Confederacy along a circular route dubbed the "Magnolia Trail."

Down the road, there are friendly people, fabulous foods and delights both natural and man-made waiting for your encounter. Enjoy!

Index

Attractions and Events

Agricultural Experiment Station (Griffin), 109
Allison Lake, 86
Amicalola Falls State Park, 49-51
Andersonville National Historic Site, 81-84
Antebellum Trail (Eatonton), 94
APEX Museum (Atlanta), 137
Appalachian Trail, 50
Arsenal Place (Columbus), 122
Atlanta Dragway, 70, 71
Atlanta History Museum, 138

Barnsley Gardens, 19-21
Barnesville Buggy Days, 109
Bellevue (LaGrange), 117-119
Martha Berry Museum (Rome), 42
Big Shanty Museum, 42
Buckhead (Atlanta), 138
Budweiser brewery (Cartersville), 42
Buena Vista, Georgia, 130-133
Butts-Mehre Heritage Hall, 75-76

Cabbage Patch Kids Hospital, 77
Carter Presidential Center, 137
Erskine Caldwell Birthplace, 127-129
Callaway Gardens, 123-126
Camp Sumter (Andersonville), 81
Cannonball House (Macon), 93
Catalpa (Newnan), 134
Center for Puppetry Arts, 139
Chastain Park (Atlanta), 139
Chateau Elan (winery), 67, 68
Chattahoochee National Forest, 47
Chattahoochee River, 77

Chattahoochee River National Recreation Area, 140
Chattahoochee Valley Art Museum (LaGrange), 136
Cheatham Hill, 41
Cherokee Festival, 18
Cherokee Rose Shooting Resort (Griffin), 109
Chestnut Mountain (winery), 66, 68
Chickamauga Battlefield Park, 22-24
Chief Vann House, 31-33
Chieftains Museum (Rome), 42
Clermont, Georgia, 77
CNN Center (Atlanta), 137
Columbus Iron Works, 122
Columbus Red Stix (baseball team), 136
Comer (railway) Shop, 58
Commerce, Georgia (outlet shops), 72-74
Commerce Factory Stores, 73, 74
Confederate Museum (Crawfordville), 62
Confederate Naval Museum (Columbus), 120-122
Consolidated Mine, 27
Crisson Mine (Dahlonega), 47

Dahlonega, Georgia, 45-47
Dahlonega Bluegrass Festival, 77
Dard Hunter Paper Museum, 140
Day Butterfly Center, 125-126
Douglass Theater (Macon), 108

Eatonton, Georgia, 94-96
Ebenezer Baptist Church, 137
Bill Elliott Racing Museum, 69-71
Etowah Indian Mounds, 25-27

INDEX

Fort Mountain, 42
Fort Valley, 108
Fox Winery (Social Circle), 108
Front Porch Music Hall (Buena Vista), 130
Fuller Gun Collection, 23

General Wheeler's Mess Tent and War of Northern Aggression Museum (Newnan), 135
Georgia Apple Festival (Ellijay), 42
Georgia Aviation Hall of Fame, 97-99
Georgia College (Milledgeville), 102
Georgia Marble Festival (Jasper), 42
Georgia Military College (Milledgeville), 102
Georgia Music Hall of Fame (Macon), 108
Georgia Mountain Fair (Hiawassee), 77
Georgia State Botanical Garden, 77
Glen-Ella Springs, 64
Gold Museum (Dahlonega), 45-47
Great Temple Mound (Ocmulgee), 101

Habersham Winery, 68
Hay House (Macon), 91-93
Helen, Georgia 77
Helen Oktoberfest, 78
Herndon Home (Atlanta), 139
High Museum of Art, 137
Horizon Theater (Atlanta), 139

Inman Park (Atlanta), 138
Institute of Paper Science and Technology, 140

Jarrell Plantation, 87, 88-90

Kennesaw Battlefield Park, 39-41
Kennesaw Mountain, 41
Kenney's Alley (Atlanta), 139

Martin Luther King, Jr. Birthplace (Atlanta), 137
Martin Luther King, Jr. Center for Nonviolent Social Change, 137
Kolb's Farm, 41

Lamar Dodd Art Center (LaGrange), 136
Sydney Lanier Cottage (Macon), 93
Lanier Raceway, 70, 71
Lake Burton, 64
Lake Lanier, 77
Lake Rabun, 64
Liberty Hall, 60-62
Little Five Points (Atlanta), 138
Little Kennesaw, 41
Little White House, 113-116
Crawford Long Museum, 55

Macon Braves (baseball team), 108
Madison, Georgia, 77
Male Academy Museum (Newnan), 134
Mark of the Potter (Sautee Valley), 77
Mark Trail Memorabilia Exhibit, 77
Massee Lane Gardens, 108
Milledgeville, Georgia, 102-104
Monastery of the Holy Spirit (Conyers), 108
Museum of Aviation (Warner Robins), 97-99
Museum and Archives of Georgia Education (Milledgeville), 104

National Country Music Hall of Fame (Buena Vista), 130
National Infantry Museum (Fort Benning), 136
National Prisoner of War Museum, 83
Navy Supply Corps Museum (Athens), 77

INDEX

New Echotah, 15-18
Newnan, Georgia, 134-135

Oak Grove (Newnan), 134
Ocmulgee National Monument, 100-101
Old Mill Museum (Moreland), 128
Opelofa Nature Trail, 101

Panola Mountain State Conservation Park, 105-107
Panther Creek, 64
Paradise Garden, 36-38
Pasaquan (Buena Vista), 131-133
Perry, Georgia, 108
Pickett's Mill, 42
Piedmont National Wildlife Refuge, 85-87
Pigeon Hill, 41
Powers Crossroads Fair (Newnan), 136
Prater's Mill Country Fair (Dalton), 42
Elvis Presley Museum (Buena Vista), 130

Reinhardt College, 42
Renaissance Faire (Fairburn), 136
River Dumpsite Gallery (Atlanta), 140
Road Atlanta (racing), 70, 71
Rock Eagle (Eatonton), 108
Franklin D. Roosevelt State Park, 116
Rural Electrification Museum, 113

St. Joseph's Catholic Church (Macon), 93
SciTrek Science Museum, 137
Sibley Horticultural Center, 123
Silver Moon Music Barn (Buena Vista), 130
Smith House (Dahlonega), 47
Southeastern Railway Museum, 58-59
Springer Mountain, 50

Alexander Stephens Home, 54, 60-62
Stone Mountain, 105
Sweetwater Creek State Park, 136

Tallulah Falls, 63-65
Tanger Outlet Mall (Commerce), 72-73, 74
Tate House, 34-35
Theater Gael (Atlanta), 139
Robert Toombs Home, 52-54, 62
Tunnel Hill, 42

Uncle Remus Museum (Eatonton), 94-96
University of Georgia (Athens), 75-76

Vann Tavern, 15
Carl Vinson Memorial Exhibit (Milledgevile), 104
Virginia-Highland (Atlanta), 138

Warm Springs, Georgia, 113-116
Weinman Mineral Museum, 28-30
West Ridge Trail (Amicalola), 49
Wine Country, 66-68
Woodruff House (Macon), 93
Worcester House, 16

Zoo Atlanta, 137